Radiology Casebook for Medical Students

Second Edition

Rema Wasan BA MBBS MA MRCP
Consultant Radiologist
King's College Hospital, London

Alan Grundy MB ChB DCH FRCR
Consultant and Senior Lecturer in Diagnostic Radiology
St George's Hospital and Medical School, London

Richard Beese BSc(Hons) MBBS MRCP FRCR
Clinical Fellow Radiology
St George's Hospital, London

PASTEST
Dedicated to your success

First published in 2000
Reprinted 2003
Second Edition 2004

ISBN 1 901198 40 5

A catalogue record for this book is available from the British Library.

The information contained within this book was obtained by the author from reliable sources. However, while every effort has been made to ensure its accuracy, no responsibility for loss, damage or injury occasioned to any person acting or refraining from action as a result of information contained herein can be accepted by the publishers or author.

PasTest Revision Books and Intensive Courses
PasTest has been established in the field of postgraduate medical education since 1972, providing revision books and intensive study courses for doctors preparing for their professional examinations.

Books and courses are available for the following specialities:
MRCP Part 1 and Part 2, MRCPCH Part 1 and Part 2, MRCOG, DRCOG, MRCGP, MRCPsych, DCH, FRCA, MRCS, PLAB.

For further details contact:
PasTest Ltd, Freepost, Knutsford, Cheshire WA16 7BR
Tel: 01565 752000   Fax: 01565 650264
Email: enquiries@pastest.co.uk   Web site:www.pastest.co.uk

Designed, typeset and printed by
Hobbs the Printers Ltd, Brunel Road, Totton, Hampshire SO40 3WX

Images are produced with the kind permission of King's College Hospital, London, and St George's Hospital, London.

CONTENTS

INTRODUCTION

This book of radiology case studies is intended to provide an introduction to radiology and an introduction to the radiological management of commonly seen clinical situations. The format used is based on tutorial material used at St. George's Hospital Medical School over the past years and also examples of the type of cases which are now being used in medical school examinations. Radiology lends itself particularly for the OSPE (Objective structured practical examination) sections of examination papers.

In addition to the case studies, we have aimed to introduce a logical approach to interpretation of chest radiographs and plain abdominal films.

We have also aimed at providing guidance on the appropriate imaging modalities for investigation of clinical problems such as haematuria, obstructive jaundice and the unconscious patient.

CHEST RADIOGRAPHS

Most chest radiographs are taken in the PA projection (posteroanterior). This is taken with the patient standing erect with the patient's chest and sternum nearest to the film; the shoulders are brought forwards so that the scapulae can be projected off the chest. The X-ray tube is behind the patient and there is little in the way of geometric magnification of the heart size on the resulting film. Not all patients, however, are able to be adequately radiographed in this position and films with the patient supine or sitting up in bed result in an AP (anteroposterior) film in which there is some magnification of the heart and mediastinum and the scapulae overlie the upper zones.

When looking at the chest radiograph in a clinical setting, it is important to check that the film is correctly labelled with the patient's name and date of the examination and on the PA film, this is by convention at the top right hand side. It is also important to check the side markers since, although rather rare, dextrocardia or situs inversus is occasionally encountered.

There is a vast amount of information on the conventional chest film and a systematic approach is needed to assess it. If the patient is well positioned with respect to the film, the medial ends of the clavicles will be seen to be equidistant from the vertebral spinous processes. If the patient is rotated to one side then the right heart border can be obscured or the mediastinum may appear unduly widened.

A systematic approach is to assess the film, taking into consideration the following points:

▋ heart size, contour and silhouette
▋ both hemidiaphragms
▋ mediastinal structures including aorta and trachea
▋ hilar regions
▋ lungs, pulmonary vessels, lung edge
▋ areas of increased opacity, nodules and masses, linear shadows
▋ loss of silhouette sign of heart mediastinum and hemidiaphragms
▋ bony structures: Ribs, vertebrae and shoulder girdle.

SILHOUETTE SIGN

The appearances of the heart, mediastinum and lungs depend mainly on the differences in trans-radiance of the air-containing lung adjacent to the soft tissues of the heart, mediastinum and pulmonary vessels. The cardiac contour is clearly seen because of aerated lung adjacent to the heart along the right heart border and left heart border.

In Fig. i the left heart border is not seen since the whole of the left lung is no longer aerated. In this patient who has recently undergone aortic valve replacement, this is due to the alveoli being full of aspirated fluid and secretions. Note the presence of metallic sternal sutures and the wire struts of the aortic replacement.

Figure i

There is aerated lung adjacent to the aorta and the main pulmonary outflow tract. The right and left hemidiaphragms are seen clearly because there is aerated lung normally in contact with the surface of the diaphragm. Aerated lung normally reaches right up to the ribs on the lateral and superior aspects of the hemithorax.

In Fig. ii there is an apical pneumothorax and the lung edge can be seen 3-4 cm away from the ribs at the apex. Pulmonary vessels are not seen in this area.

The transverse diameter of the heart is normally less than 50% of the maximum transverse diameter of the chest taken from the inner margins of the ribs laterally at their widest point. The heart looks larger on supine or AP films. The right heart border is made up superiorly of the superior vena cava and the right atrium which are separated by the pericardium and pleura from the right middle lobe. The left heart border is seen in its lower portion because of normal aerated lung of the lingular lobe and superiorly the left heart border is made up of

Figure ii

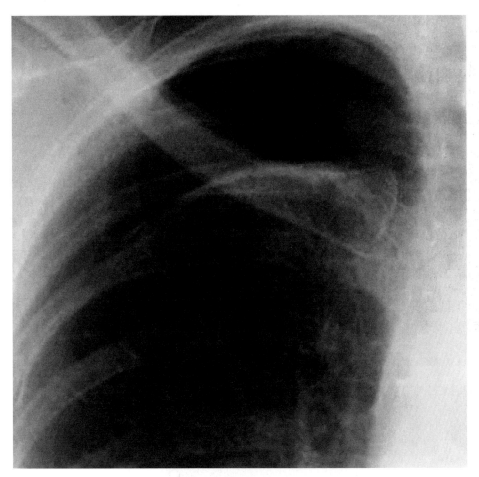

the main pulmonary outflow tract and the aortic knuckle. These are clearly seen because there is aerated lung in the left upper lobe.

MEDIASTINUM AND HILA

The trachea is seen as an air-filled structure lying centrally, although it is often displaced slightly to the right by the aorta, particularly in older patients. A good quality radiograph should allow the right and left main bronchi to be visible and the normal carinal angle between the right and left main bronchi should be less than 90°. The hila are made up of the pulmonary arteries and pulmonary veins and the bronchi at the root of the lung. The right hemidiaphragm is usually slightly higher than the left.

LUNGS

Within the lungs the only structures which are clearly visible are the pulmonary arteries and veins and these are normally seen to extend as far as the outer third of the lung parenchyma. The lower zone vessels are usually slightly more prominent than the upper zone vessels on the PA film as a result of the normal differential blood flow. The lung edge cannot be seen in the normal patient since it is in contact with the chest wall and can only be seen in the presence of a pneumothorax. The fissures separating the left upper and lower lobes and the right upper, middle and lower lobes are not usually visible with the exception of the horizontal fissure on the right which extends from the right hilum to the chest wall and marks the upper border of the right middle lobe.

BONES AND SOFT TISSUES

Bony structures, including the ribs, clavicles and usually the shoulder girdle are visible on the PA film and attention should be paid to these. Overlying soft tissue abnormalities may occasionally cause confusion. In the female the breasts may produce significant soft tissue shadowing over the lower zones and occasionally nipple shadows may be mistaken for a pulmonary lesion.

Abnormalities that should be looked for on a chest X-ray are increase in the heart size, loss of the normal silhouette of the cardiac contour (Fig. i) or diaphragm due to the absence of aerated lung adjacent to these structures, areas of increased density, rounded lesions and linear shadows.

CONSOLIDATION

Consolidation is the term used to describe a section of lung or an entire lobe or occasionally a whole lung where the alveoli are no longer aerated. In this situation they may be filled either with fluid, pus, tumour cells or even blood.

Figure iii

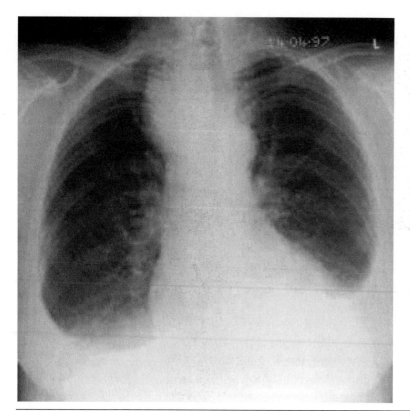

It is not possible on the chest X-ray to determine the nature of the material which has replaced the air. One feature of consolidated lung is that the major airways into the affected area may still contain air and this appearance is termed an air bronchogram. Fluid in the pleural space, if of a small quality, is seen as blunting of the costophrenic angles (Fig. iii), but more extensive fluid will produce an opacity of the lower zones or even complete opacification of the hemithorax. It is not possible radiologically to differentiate between pleural transudates, exudates, blood or chyle within the pleural space.

MASSES AND NODULES

When assessing rounded lesions the important points are:

▌ the size of a lesion
▌ the contour: Is it well defined or are the edges indistinct or spiculated?
▌ the number of lesions: Single or multiple
▌ the density: Soft tissue or is there calcification present?

Figure iv shows a well defined mass lesion in the right upper zone abutting the right side of the superior mediastinum. The right hilar vessels are also not seen through the mass and there is a small pocket of air within the mass indicating that the mass is cavitating. Multiple small rounded opacities scattered throughout both lungs are often described as miliary opacities.

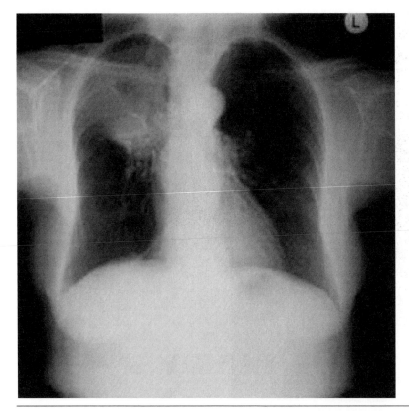

Figure iv

THE ABDOMINAL RADIOGRAPH

The abdominal radiograph is usually taken with the patient supine. Erect films of the abdomen are of little value and many radiology departments do not take erect films as a matter of principle. It is only in cases of bowel obstruction that the erect film may be of any value and even in this situation supine film will give enough information for a confident clinical diagnosis. The interpretation of the abdominal film should be done in a systematic manner.

The main features to look at are:

▊ bowel gas pattern
▊ soft tissues, soft tissue masses and fat planes
▊ areas of calcification
▊ bony structures.

BOWEL GAS PATTERN

On the abdominal film gas within the lumen of loops of bowel allows the bowel to be identified. There is normally gas in the stomach and large amounts in the colon and rectum. There is not much gas in the small bowel. The position of the gas-filled loops helps identify which part of bowel one is looking at. Ascending and descending colon are normally the

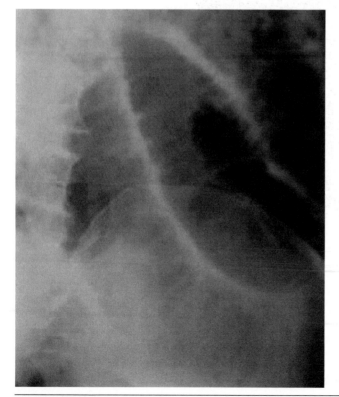

Figure v

most laterally seen loops of bowel. The transverse colon can be identified crossing the upper part of the abdomen although it can reach down into the pelvis. Air in the rectum can usually be seen in the midline in the pelvis. Small bowel tends to lie centrally and the stomach can be seen in the left upper abdomen crossing to the right. Faecal matter is usually present in the large bowel and recto-sigmoid. The characteristic mucosal fold pattern of the small bowel is clearly seen, particularly when there is distension of bowel loops. The valvulae conniventes are seen as parallel bands extending fully across the lumen of the small bowel. In the proximal small bowel they are close together and the distance between folds increases towards the distal ileum where the folds may be up to 1 cm apart.

In Fig. v there is a dilated loop of bowel measuring 5 cm in diameter. Mucosal folds can clearly be seen extending across the entire lumen indicating that this is small bowel. The inter-haustral folds in the large bowel by contrast do not reach across the full diameter of the bowel.

Figure vi shows a dilated loop of large bowel with the haustral folds only extending one third of the way across the lumen (arrows).The calibre of the bowel varies quite considerably due to peristaltic activity. Small bowel is abnormal if the loops are greater than 3 cm diameter and in the transverse colon a diameter of 5.5 cm is taken as the upper limit of normal.

Figure vi

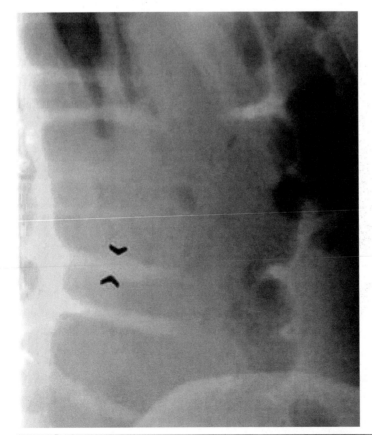

Figure vii

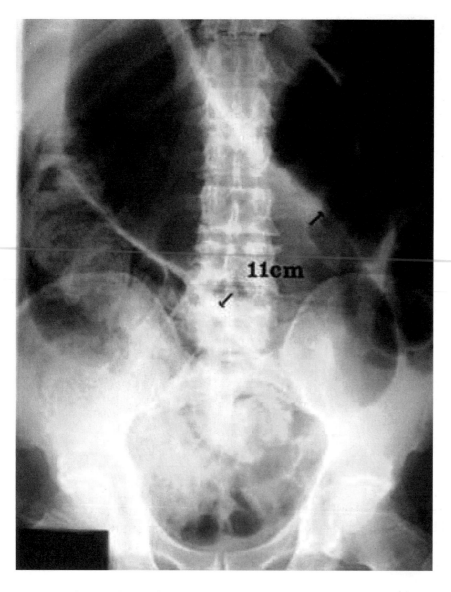

11cm

Figure vii shows a loop of bowel measuring 11 cm in diameter. Although there are no mucosal folds visible, this is a grossly distended loop of sigmoid colon in a patient with a sigmoid volvulus. Any abnormal position of bowel loops should be noted and in particular the area beneath the superior pubic ramus where inguinal and femoral herniae are found. Air seen outside the bowel lumen is abnormal. Free intraperitoneal air can be recognised and air in other structures such as the biliary tree or urinary bladder may be seen on the abdominal film.

In cases of suspected bowel perforation the best film for diagnostic purposes is the erect chest X-ray (Fig. viii) which may show air beneath the diaphragm. In this case a crescent of air can be seen lying under the right hemidiaphragm and the upper surface of the liver (arrows).

Figure viii

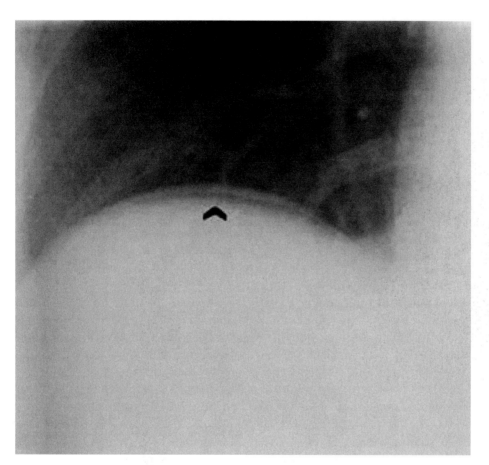

SOFT TISSUES

The lower border of the liver can usually be identified and both kidneys may be seen because of the lower density perirenal fat surrounding them. The tip of the spleen may be identifiable. A full bladder may be seen in the pelvis. Along both sides of the lumbar spine the lateral margin of the psoas muscle can be seen. Other structures such as the pancreas, adrenals, ovaries and uterus cannot be separately identified.

CALCIFIED STRUCTURES

Costal cartilage calcification is a normal finding and can be identified projected over the upper abdomen. Calcification in abdominal vessels, especially the aorta and iliac arteries and splenic artery, is often seen in elderly patients. Calcification in other sites is always pathological.

BONES

An assessment of the bony structures must be included. Pathology may be present in the ribs, vertebral column, iliac crests, pubic rami and femoral heads. The sacroiliac joint may be abnormal in patients with inflammatory bowel disease. Bony metastases may easily be overlooked.

BOWEL OBSTRUCTION

Small bowel obstruction (Fig. v)

With the onset of obstruction there is a halt to the onward passage of bowel content and the bowel proximal to an obstructing lesion becomes distended with bowel contents (fluid and air). Distal to an obstruction peristaltic activity continues and the bowel will eventually empty and become collapsed down. The diagnosis of small bowel obstruction is based on identification of dilated bowel loops proximal to the site of obstruction. The fold patterns of the bowel loops, and to some extent the position of loops, enables the differentiation of large from small bowel. Small bowel distension greater than 3 cm is considered abnormal. In the normal situation there is little air in the small bowel and in the presence of small bowel obstruction a large amount of air may be seen. If the site of obstruction is high in the jejunum and the patient has been vomiting this may not, however, be apparent. In most cases of small bowel obstruction the cause cannot be ascertained from the plain film.

Large bowel obstruction (Figs. vi & vii)

In the normal colon the contents in the right side of the colon are still fairly liquid and only in the left side of the colon and the sigmoid colon do solid faeces form as water is reabsorbed. There is normally air throughout the colon and rectum. Following onset of large bowel obstruction there is an accumulation of air and faecal matter proximal to the lesion and distal to the lesion the colon is empty. Some residual air may, however, be seen in the rectum in the presence of a large bowel obstruction. The normal colon is up 5.5 cm diameter. The degree of distension that can occur in the colon depends on the integrity of the ileo-caecal valve.

A competent valve prevents decompression of the colon into the small bowel and in this situation the caecum may become excessively distended. Danger of ischaemia of the wall occurs if the colon becomes excessively dilated and a caecum greater than 8 cm in diameter is in danger of perforation. If the ileo-caecal valve is incompetent them the colon will be allowed to decompress to some extent and the small bowel will also become distended. In cases of large and small bowel obstruction it is important to remember to look at the area under the superior pubic ramus for evidence of a femoral or inguinal hernia.

Further radiological investigation of large bowel obstruction can be performed. A barium enema can be performed safely provided there is no suggestion of large bowel perforation and may be useful in demonstrating the exact site and cause of large bowel obstruction to allow the surgeon to plan the surgery more appropriately.

Chapter 1
ABDOMEN

A 75-year-old man presents with a history of attacks of central colicky abdominal pain lasting for two to three minutes at a time. He vomited after the first bout of pain but has not vomited since. On examination his abdomen is distended slightly and he is dehydrated with a dry tongue and dry skin. Tinkling bowel sounds are heard. On rectal examination the rectum is empty. Hernial orifices are normal. A right paramedian scar is noted. A supine abdominal film is obtained.

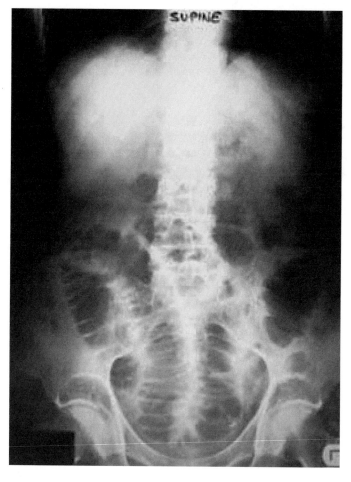

Figure 1

A   *Is this small or large bowel obstruction?*
B   *What is the most likely cause of the obstruction?*

Answer

A

The history suggests bowel obstruction. The supine film shows dilated loops of bowel measuring about 5 cm in diameter situated centrally in the abdomen and lying more or less transversely. Mucosal folds can be seen extending all the way across the lumen of the distended loops indicating that this is small bowel. No gas or faeces are seen in the large bowel or rectum. There is no evidence of bowel gas in the region of the inguinal hernial orifices. These appearances are in keeping with a small bowel obstruction. The relatively large number of small bowel loops visible would suggest a **distal small bowel** obstruction. In this case there are no other radiological signs to suggest the cause of the obstruction.

B

Clinical examination had revealed a surgical scar and adhesions from previous surgery were thought to be the cause of his obstruction. Adhesions from previous surgery are one of the most common causes of small bowel obstruction. The patient was managed conservatively and the obstruction settled.

Answer overleaf

This 85-year-old lady has a three day history of central colicky abdominal pain, has not vomited but has stopped eating and drinking. She has complained of fatty intolerance over many years but has not been investigated. She has not had any previous surgery or interventional procedures. On examination she is dehydrated, has a tachycardia and low blood pressure. Examination of her abdomen shows moderate distension and few bowel sounds. No masses are palpable and hernia orifices are normal. There are no abdominal scars and her rectum contains a small amount of faeces. The supine abdominal film is shown below.

Figure 2

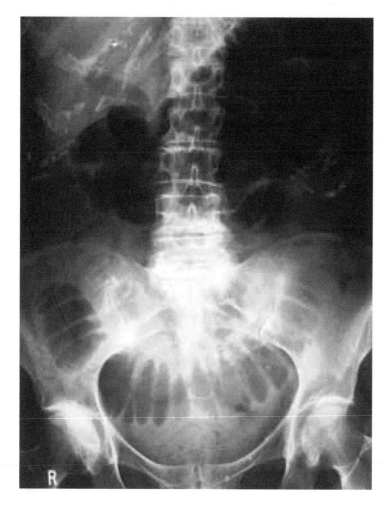

A   *Is the distended loop in the lower part of the abdomen small or large bowel?*
B   *The stomach is also filled with air; is this usual in obstruction?*
C   *Is there an indication of the cause of obstruction from this film?*

Answer

A
The dilated loop of bowel lying transversely in the lower abdomen has mucosal folds across the full width of the loop indicating that this is **small bowel.**

B
The gaseous distension of the stomach seen in the upper abdomen is unusual; in most cases of small bowel obstruction the stomach is empty since the patient has usually been vomiting.

C
A clue to the cause of this lady's obstruction is seen in the right hypochondrium where air can be observed in the common bile duct and to a lesser extent in branching intrahepatic ducts.

This is a case of **gallstone ileus.** Gallstone ileus occurs when a large gallstone has ulcerated through the gall bladder wall into an adjacent adherent loop of small bowel. It continues through the small bowel to become impacted in the terminal ileum, producing an obstruction. The typical appearances of small bowel obstruction are seen but since there is a fistula between the gall bladder and small bowel, air from the bowel passes through this and becomes visible in the biliary tree.

This obese 55-year-old patient presents with a history of central colicky abdominal pain, vomiting and clinical signs of small bowel obstruction.

Figure 3

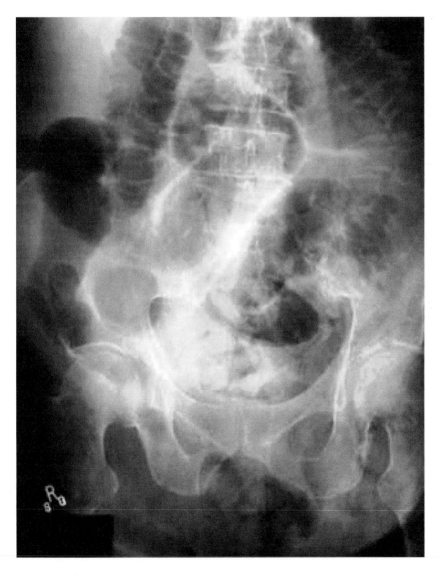

A   *Are there any loops of bowel in an abnormal situation which might indicate a cause for the obstruction?*

Answer

A

In addition to dilated loops of small bowel centrally in the abdomen there are air filled bowel shadows seen lying inferior to the superior pubic rami. This is bowel in **bilateral inguinal herniae.** In patients who are obese it may be difficult clinically to detect a hernia and the presence of bowel gas in relation to hernial orifices may indicate an obstructed hernia. The abdominal film in general only shows evidence of obstruction and only in cases such as gallstone ileus or hernia obstruction can the cause be suggested from the plain film. When considering the cause of any obstruction of any tubular structure, whether it be a segment of bowel, a ureter, a vein or artery, lymphatic vessels or even salivary ducts, it is worth classifying the causes according to the situation of the obstructing lesion. Is it:

■ within the lumen?
■ arising within the wall?
■ extrinsic to the structure?

In considering the cause of small bowel obstruction, intraluminal causes include the gallstone of gallstone ileus and ingested foreign bodies. Pathology arising in the wall of the small bowel giving rise to obstruction includes inflammatory conditions such as Crohn's disease and tumours such as lymphoma. Of the extrinsic processes, adhesion bands from previous surgery and hernias are the most common causes of obstruction.

A 74-year-old lady gives a history of lower abdominal colicky pain and increasing constipation for five days. She has not been vomiting but has become increasingly distended over the past two days. She admits to having noticed some fresh blood mixed with stool on several occasions in the past three months. She also gives a history of exertional dyspnoea for one month. She has undergone a hip replacement some years previously and this can be clearly seen on the film. On examination her abdomen is distended with few bowel sounds. There are no abdominal scars. Rectal examination reveals an empty rectum. An abdominal film is taken.

Figure 4a

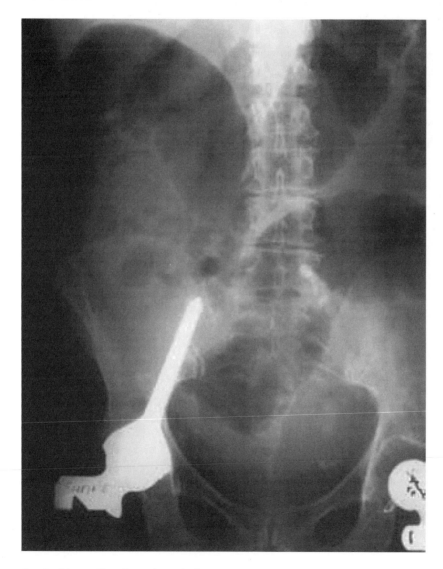

A *Is this small or large bowel obstruction?*
B *What further radiological investigation may be carried out to confirm this?*

Answer

A

There is distension of loops of bowel, some more than 6 cm in diameter. Prominent haustral folds are seen which extend only partially across the bowel lumen indicating that this is **large bowel.** There are mottled gas shadows in the right iliac fossa which represent semi-liquid faecal matter in the caecum. There is no evidence of distended small bowel. There is absence of gas and faeces in the rectum and no gas is seen in the left iliac fossa. These appearances are consistent with a large bowel obstruction. Since colonic gas can be seen as far as the descending colon, the obstruction must be distal to this point.

Figure 4b

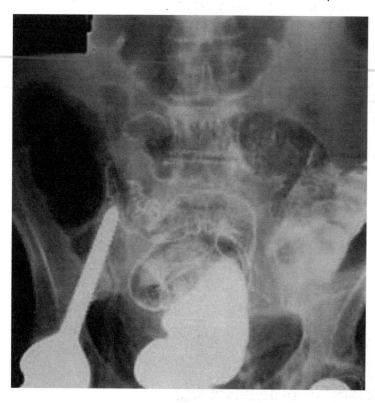

B

A barium enema was carried out without any bowel preparation and revealed a tight obstructing lesion in the sigmoid colon with shouldered edges and a narrow lumen in keeping with a sigmoid carcinoma.

This elderly man gives a history of several days' constipation and lower abdominal colicky pain. He has become distended and noticed that his trousers are now too tight around the waist. On examination his abdomen is distended with a few high pitched bowel sounds. His supine abdominal film is shown.

Figure 5

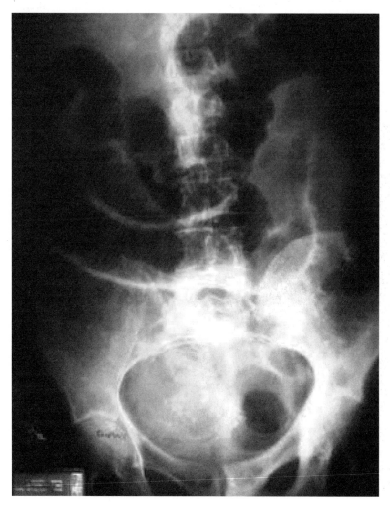

A   *What parts of the bowel are distended?*
B   *Why is the large bowel distension not prominent?*

Answer

A

In this case there is prominent s**mall bowel distension**: Centrally placed loops which show mucosal folds all the way across the bowel loops. Loops of large bowel are, however, seen in the right side and across the upper part of the abdomen but these loops are not as distended as in the previous case. The ileo-caecal valve is incompetent in this patient and the large bowel has been able to decompress into the small bowel. The presence of large bowel gas differentiates this from a small bowel obstruction in which the large bowel should be empty of gas and faeces. Subsequent barium enema examination also showed a carcinoma in the sigmoid colon.

B

It is unusual to be able to identify the underlying pathology causing large bowel obstruction apart from sigmoid volvulus. As with small bowel obstruction, it is worthwhile considering whether the cause is intraluminal, mural or extrinsic. The most common causes of large bowel obstruction are processes arising primarily in the wall of the colon. Colorectal malignancy, particularly left-sided lesions and diverticular disease, are the most common causes of large bowel obstruction.

Answer overleaf

An 82-year-old man gives a long history of repeated attacks of acute left-sided abdominal pain that has been terminated by the passage of large quantities of flatus and faeces. On this occasion, the onset of left-sided pain occurred while the patient was straining at passing a stool. He did not empty his bowel nor pass any flatus and has developed considerable distension of the abdomen over a period of five to six hours. He complains of hiccoughing and retching but has not vomited and has still not passed any flatus or stools. A plain abdominal film is taken.

Figure 6

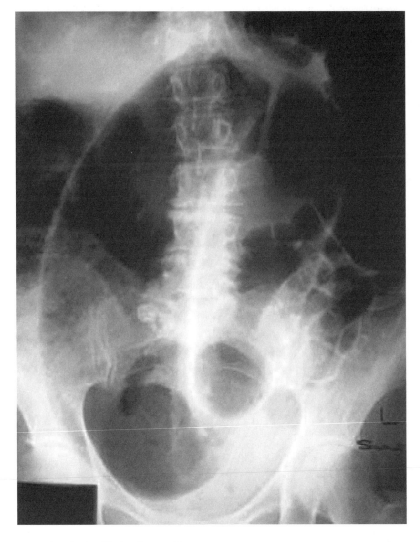

A   *What is the likely diagnosis?*
B   *What further procedure may be carried out?*

Answer

A

The abdominal film shows a very large distended loop of bowel lying centrally in the abdomen. No mucosal folds can be seen to help distinguish between large and small bowel. Some air and faecal matter is seen in the right side of the colon and also across the transverse colon and in the region of the hepatic flexure. Small bowel distension is not seen. This distended loop is sigmoid colon. When the sigmoid colon becomes massively distended the haustral pattern can be completely obliterated. This appearance is typical of a sigmoid volvulus. In **sigmoid volvulus** the sigmoid colon twists around the mesentery producing a closed loop obstruction.

The closed loop of sigmoid colon becomes grossly distended with air. As the sigmoid dilates the haustral pattern may become completely lost and the resulting loop of dilated bowel becomes featureless. Since the colon proximal to the sigmoid is also obstructed, distension of the rest of the colon is seen.

Typically these patients have a considerable amount of faecal loading proximal to the sigmoid loop. Although the typical appearance of a sigmoid volvulus is of the dilated loop arising from the left iliac fossa and resembling a coffee bean, any patient in whom a very large dilated featureless loop of air filled bowel is seen should be considered as having a sigmoid volvulus.

B

The next procedure should be flexible sigmoidoscopy. The instrument can be passed into the distended sigmoid loop allowing the gas to escape and the volvulus to reduce. An instant barium enema may also be used to confirm the diagnosis and the procedure may result in untwisting of the sigmoid colon with expulsion of a large quantity of air and faecal matter. If the volvulus can be reduced by either of these means the patient's clinical condition can be improved and surgery considered at a later date.

Answer
overleaf

A 30-year-old man gives a history of epigastric pain waking him at night over the past three weeks. The pain is relieved by drinking a glass of milk. On this occasion he had sudden onset of severe epigastric pain in the early morning and the pain rapidly spread to involve the whole abdomen. The pain is aggravated by movement, coughing and deep breathing. On examination he is pale and sweating; he is not shocked. Breathing is shallow and rapid. Abdominal examination reveals rigidity and extreme tenderness over the epigastrium; bowel sounds are not heard. An erect chest X-ray is obtained.

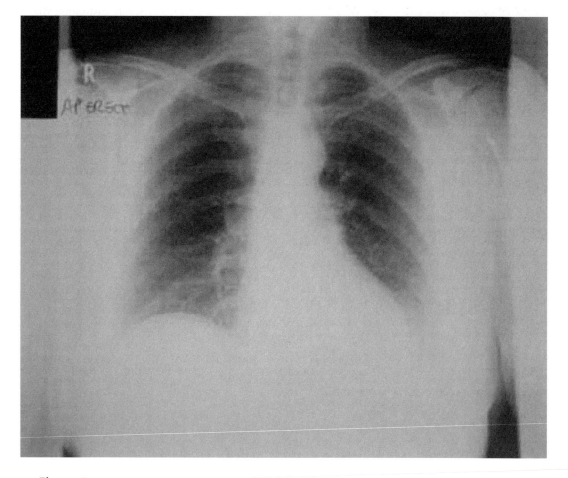

Figure 7

A *What is the likely diagnosis?*
B *Are there signs on the film to confirm this?*

Answer

A

The clinical picture is typical of a **perforated duodenal ulcer.** In cases of perforation of the bowel, the appropriate radiograph to obtain is an erect chest film. Perforation of the gut allows intestinal contents to enter into the peritoneal cavity and it is the air from within the gut lumen that produces the radiological appearances. With the patient in the erect position, any air extravasated from the gut lumen will rise to the highest point in the peritoneal cavity; in the erect position this is immediately under the diaphragm.

B

On this erect film, air can be seen as a thin lucent line parallel to the right hemidiaphragm. Free air is not seen in all cases of perforation. A localised perforation into the lesser sac will not produce a generalised pneumoperitoneum. This small amount of air is enough to confirm the clinical diagnosis of a perforation.

This 67-year-old patient gives a history of sudden onset of lower chest pain which is thought initially to be cardiac in origin; an erect chest radiograph is obtained.

Figure 8

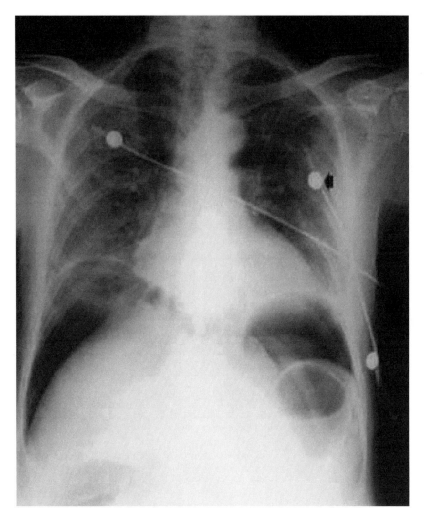

A   *Is there free air in the peritoneal cavity?*
B   *What is the arrow pointing at?*
C   *What two conditions should be considered in this case?*

Answer

A

In this case there is a large amount of air beneath both hemidiaphragms. When there is a large amount of free air it may be mistaken for air within the colon. However no colonic mucosal fold pattern can be seen immediately beneath the diaphragm and the upper surface of the liver can clearly be seen outlined by free air.

B

The arrow is pointing at an **electrocardiograph electrode.**

C

The most common perforations encountered are **perforation of a peptic ulcer** and **perforation of a diverticulum of the sigmoid colon**. Although an inflamed appendix may perforate it is unusual to see a large amount of free intraperitoneal air. Perforation of part of the gut produces generalised peritonitis and, although the clinical history may give a clue as to the cause, the plain film is unable to give an indication as to the part of gut involved. In this case surgery confirmed a **perforated sigmoid diverticulum**.

Other causes of free intraperitoneal air must be remembered. Any patient who has recently undergone abdominal surgery will have some residual free air in the peritoneal cavity and this may take up to a week to be fully reabsorbed. Any patient having undergone any laparoscopic procedure will have free air in the peritoneum.

Answer
overleaf

Mrs J presents to casualty with an eight-hour history of sudden onset of right subcostal pain radiating around the right side to the back. She has vomited on several occasions. She gives a history of intolerance to fatty foods and flatulence after meals for several months. On examination she is very tender in the right hypochondrium and has a positive Murphy's sign. She is pyrexial but is not clinically jaundiced and her white cell count is elevated. Initially she is given 100 mg pethidine intramuscularly and later an ultrasound scan of her abdomen is performed.

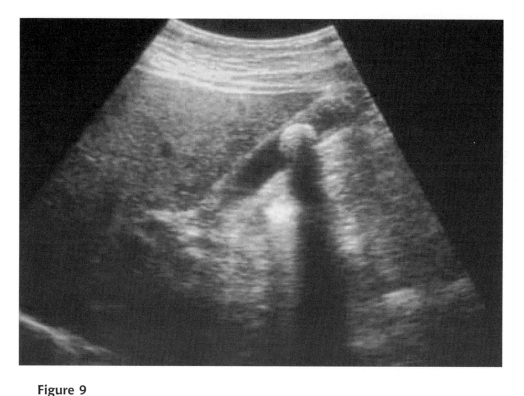

Figure 9

A   *What does this scan show?*

Answer

A

In patients suspected of having biliary disease the initial imaging should be an ultrasound scan of the upper abdomen. In this case of acute cholecystitis the scan shows the gall bladder containing a **calculus**. In addition there is some free fluid around the gall bladder. The hyperechoic calculus is seen in a dependent position in the fluid-filled gall bladder and casts an acoustic shadow behind it.

Ultrasound examination of the biliary system is now the imaging modality of choice in the initial assessment of patients with biliary disease. Calculi within the gall bladder and also within the common bile duct may be demonstrated and in addition thickening of the gall bladder wall and peri-cholecystic fluid may at times be seen, indicating acute cholecystitis.

Answer
overleaf

Mrs M has noticed that over several days her stools have become pale and her urine
has become darker. She has lost her appetite and also complains of a dull ache in the
right hypochondrium. She has had an episode of acute cholecystitis ten years earlier.
On examination her abdomen is not distended and there is no localised tenderness.
She is noted to be jaundiced with yellow sclerae and a pale yellow tinge to the skin.
Biochemistry confirmed that she has jaundice with an obstructive pattern. An ultrasound
scan of the upper abdomen is obtained.

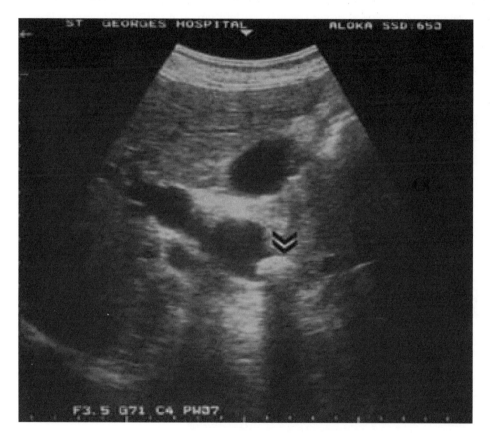

Figure 10a

A   *What is the hyperechoic structure indicated by the double arrow?*
B   *The diameter of the common bile duct is 12 mm; is this abnormal?*

Answer

A

The hyperechoic structure is a **stone** at the **lower end** of a dilated common bile duct. This produces an acoustic shadow behind the stone.

B

The common bile duct is 12 mm diameter which is abnormal. The normal diameter is less than 7 mm.

The further management of this patient consisted of endoscopic retrograde cholangio-pancreatography (ERCP). Contrast introduced into the common bile duct confirmed the presence of a calculus in the duct.

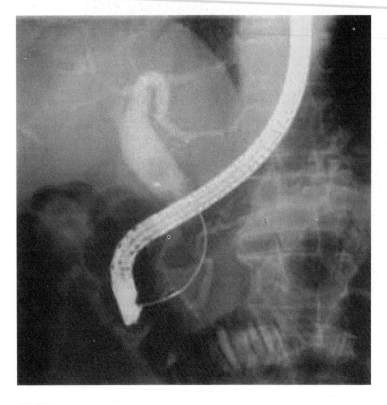

Figure 10b

An endoscopic sphincterotomy was performed and the calculus removed from the duct.

A 76-year-old man presents to his general practitioner with a history of loss of appetite for the past month and loss of weight of 5 kg. He has noticed a change in the colour of his skin and has started itching. He had a partial gastrectomy 25 years ago for peptic ulcer disease. On examination he is deeply jaundiced and there are scratch marks over his upper abdomen. There is an upper midline scar from previous surgery. He is referred for an urgent surgical opinion and an ultrasound of the upper abdomen is performed.

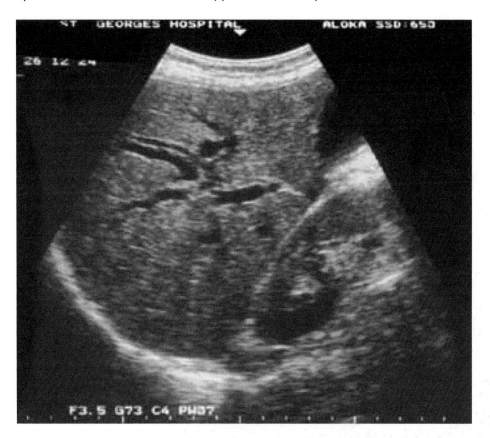

Figure 11a

A   *Is obstructive jaundice confirmed by this ultrasound scan?*

Answer

A

The ultrasound scan shows very dilated intrahepatic ducts and a dilated common bile duct. A mass was also seen at the lower end of the bile duct consistent with a pancreatic lesion.

An ERCP was not obtained since access to the second part of the duodenum was not possible due to his previous partial gastrectomy and gastroenterostomy. He was referred for a percutaneous transhepatic cholangiogram which demonstrated an extrinsic obstruction of the lower end of the common bile duct consistent with a pancreatic mass.

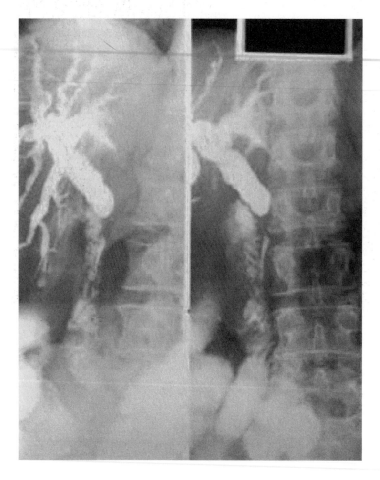

Figure 11b

Further management of the patient included a CT scan of the abdomen and a CT- guided needle biopsy of the pancreatic mass. This confirmed a pancreatic carcinoma. The CT scan showed that the tumour was invading the coeliac vessels and would not be resectable. Subsequently a biliary endoprosthesis was inserted percutaneously.

Three years ago this patient had a left hemicolectomy for a carcinoma of the descending colon. He presented 10 days ago with increasing jaundice and weight loss. On examination, as well as being jaundiced, his liver is palpable beneath the right costal margin.
A CT examination of the upper abdomen was obtained.

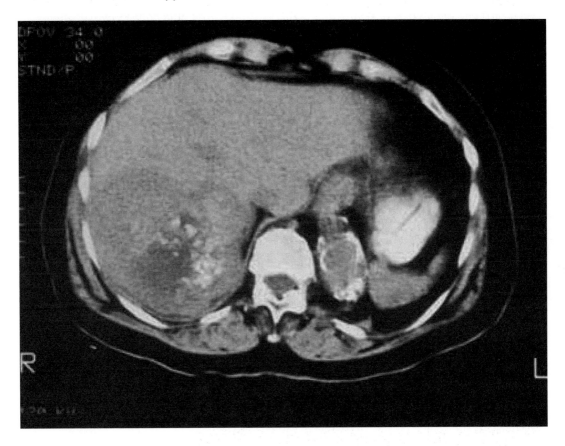

Figure 12

A   What does the CT scan show?
B   Why are the liver lesions of high density?

Answer

A

The CT scan shows a non enhancing 4cm diameter irregular lesion in the right lobe of the liver which has some areas of higher attenuation within it. The appearances are consistant with metastasis.

B

These high density areas are calcification in the centre of the metastases. The ultrasound appearances of hyperechoic-rounded lesions are typical of metastatic deposits in the liver. The corresponding low density lesions with calcification seen on the CT are consistent with metastases from colorectal carcinoma which are frequently seen to contain calcification on CT scanning. This scan has been obtained without intravenous contrast enhancement.

Investigation of obstructive jaundice

Once a diagnosis of obstructive jaundice has been made by clinical and biochemical means, the most appropriate initial imaging is an ultrasound scan of the upper abdomen. Although plain abdominal films may show the presence of calcified gallstones, only about 25% are sufficiently calcified to be visible.

Ultrasound is able to demonstrate dilatation of both the intrahepatic ducts and the extrahepatic biliary tree. Calculi in the gall bladder and duct system can be identified. Mass lesions in the head of the pancreas can also be clearly seen. Ultrasound may also readily demonstrate liver metastases.

Occasionally, however, the lower end of the common bile duct is obscured by air in the duodenal loop and it is not possible to determine the cause of obstruction.

Further demonstration of the biliary tree can be obtained from either endoscopic retrograde cholangiography (ERCP) or percutaneous transhepatic cholangiography. ERCP is the preferred procedure since endoscopic sphincterotomy and stone extraction can be performed at the same time or in cases of malignant obstruction stenting can be carried out. There are, however, circumstances in which ERCP is not practical such as where there has been previous gastric surgery and the second part of the duodenum cannot be accessed.

Occasionally at ERCP the common bile duct cannot be cannulated. In this situation the patient may go on to have a percutaneous procedure. Transhepatic cholangiography also allows the introduction of drainage catheters into the biliary tree to relieve obstruction and also allows access for the introduction of an endoprosthesis or biliary stent. The cytological examination of bile obtained at either ERCP or transhepatic cholangiography may allow a diagnosis of malignant disease to be obtained.

Further assessment of patients with obstructive jaundice before definitive surgery includes the use of CT scanning to assess invasion of adjacent structures from pancreatic tumours and an evaluation of whether tumours are resectable.

Answer overleaf

Mr K is a 23-year-old man who complains of severe pains starting in the left loin and radiating around the flank and down into his left testis. The bouts of pain last for about three minutes and are associated with sweating and vomiting. The pain has recurred several times over the past few hours. On examination he is not in pain at the time. Urine testing is positive for a small amount of blood. A plain abdominal film is taken.

Figure 13a

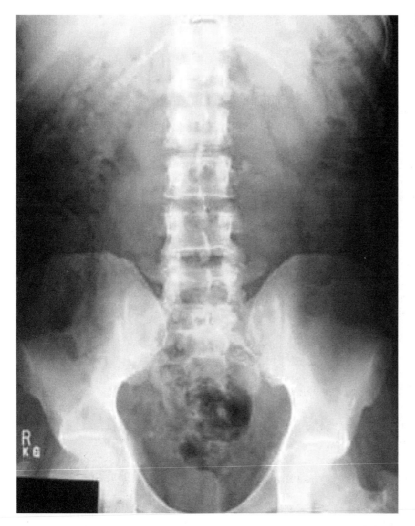

A   *What does this show?*
B   *What further radiological investigation would confirm this?*

Answer

A
The plain abdominal film shows 3 mm opacity to the left of the body of the second lumbar vertebra. This is suggestive of a calculus in the left ureter causing his renal colic.

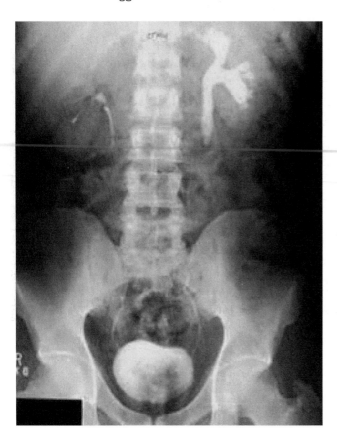

Figure 13b

B
This should be confirmed by obtaining an intravenous urogram (IVU). The film shown was obtained 15 minutes after intravenous contrast injection and shows normal excretion on the right with non-dilated renal pelvis and ureter. On the left there is retention of contrast within the collecting tubules of the kidney producing a dense nephrogram. There is also some opacification of a dilated renal pelvis and upper ureter as far down as the opacity seen on the plain film. Distal to this, the ureter is of normal calibre. This confirms a ureteric calculus producing obstruction to flow of urine on this side.

Answer
overleaf

A 57-year-old man complains of a five-week history of pain in the right hypochondrium and of passing frank blood in his urine on several occasions. He has not noticed a reduction in the stream of urine and has not complained of any other urinary symptoms. Examination of urine confirms the presence of red cells. He attends the 'one-stop haematuria clinic' and has an ultrasound and intravenous urogram performed. An ultrasound scan of the right kidney and a 15 minute film from an intravenous urogram (IVU) are shown.

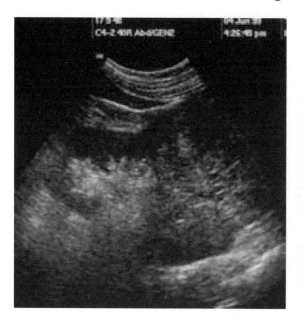

Figure 14a

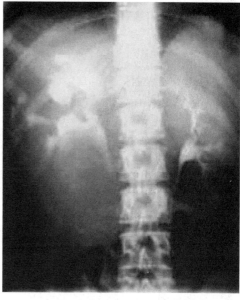

Figure 14b

A   *What does the ultrasound scan show?*
B   *Is this confirmed by the IVU?*

Answer

A

In this case the ultrasound scan (Fig 14a) has revealed a mass lesion at the lower pole of the right kidney. The urogram (Fig 14b) shows expansion of the lower pole of the right kidney with distortion and distension of the upper pole calyces and collecting system. The mass was biopsied under ultrasound guidance and histological examination showed it to be a **renal cell carcinoma**.

Further assessment of the patient with a renal cell carcinoma will include a CT scan of the abdomen to assess invasion of adjacent structures and spread of tumour into the renal vein and inferior vena cava and to assess whether regional lymph nodes have become involved. Chest radiograph is also necessary to exclude metastatic spread to the lung.

Haematuria is a symptom that must not be ignored. In the investigation of haematuria ultrasound is used to look at the kidneys and bladder. Dilatation of the renal collecting systems (hydronephrosis) can easily be demonstrated. Ultrasound of the urinary bladder can show bladder wall thickening and the presence of intravesical masses.

B

The intravenous urogram is used to visualise the renal outlines and the collecting systems including the ureters and the bladder. Significant-sized bladder tumours can be present and not seen on urography.

If ultrasound and an IVU fail to show a cause for haematuria, it is essential that the patient is referred for cystoscopic examination. Haematuria from prostatic disease and bladder tumours cannot reliably be excluded by ultrasound or intravenous urography.

Answer overleaf

This patient gives a history of having noticed blood in his urine on several occasions over a period of three months. An IVU is performed as an out-patient. The 15 minute film is shown.

Figure 15

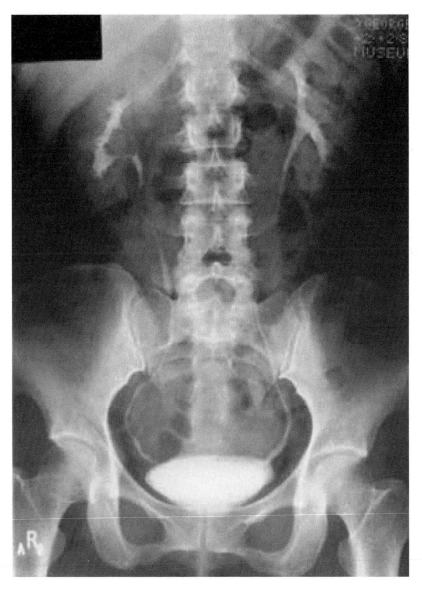

A   *Are the collecting systems normal?*

Answer

The IVU film in this patient shows contrast outlining a 2 cm diameter filling defect in the right renal pelvis. The right renal pelvis is well filled with contrast.

The differential diagnosis of a filling defect in the renal collecting system includes a calculus, transitional cell carcinoma, renal cell carcinoma, blood clot and fungal infections. Cytological examination of urine showed that this was a transitional cell carcinoma.

A 49-year-old man has been referred to the urology clinic by his GP. He complains of haematuria. He has lived abroad for many years but is now settled in the UK.

Figure 16

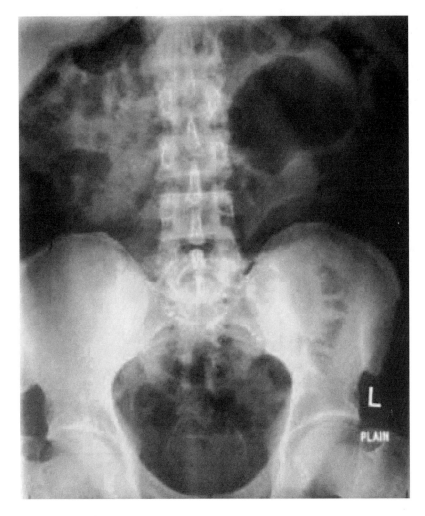

A *What is the name of the X-ray that includes the entire renal tract? How does it differ from an abdominal X-ray?*
B *What is the abnormality on the film?*
C *What is the diagnosis?*

Answer

A

KUB ie to include the **K**idney, **U**reter and **B**ladder.
The KUB includes a larger area than a standard abdominal film.

B

There is a thin rim of calcification in the bladder.

C

The diagnosis is **schistosomiasis**.

A 67-year-old lady complains of noticing blood mixed with stool on several occasions over a period of approximately five weeks; she is otherwise fit and well. She is not anaemic and there are no physical findings on examination. A flexible sigmoidoscopy in the out-patients department has shown no abnormality but stool samples are positive for blood. She is reluctant to undergo colonoscopy and a barium enema is performed. This is one of the series of films taken of the descending colon.

Figure 17

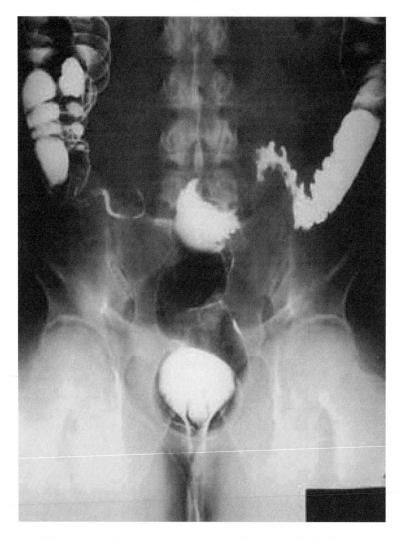

A   *What are the characteristic radiological features of the lesion in the descending colon?*

Answer

A

There is a circumferential narrowed segment in the sigmoid colon. The mucosa appears to have been destroyed in this segment and there is some shouldering of the proximal and distal margins of the narrowed segment, giving the 'apple-core' appearance. This is a typical appearance of a carcinoma of the colon. Carcinomas of the colon are either circumferential lesions such as this or polypoid masses. Those on the left side tend to be circumferential while those in the right side of the colon have a tendency to be polyploid.

Carcinomas on the left side of the colon are more likely to present with overt blood mixed with stool or as a case of large bowel obstruction. Right side tumours often present with iron deficiency anaemia due to occult bleeding.

In the patient presenting with rectal bleeding with positive faecal occult blood, the choice of investigation is between a barium enema examination and fibre-optic endoscopy. The use of flexible sigmoidoscopy in the out-patient department will identify most tumours in the recto-sigmoid colon. More proximal tumours will only be demonstrated either on full colonoscopy or barium enema.

The decision as to whether to proceed to barium enema or colonoscopy is often made on the basis of availability. Both barium enema and colonoscopy require an empty colon which is achieved by a 24-hour regime of aperients and a liquid diet. Colonoscopy has the advantage of being able to biopsy lesions at the time of the investigation.

A 74-year-old lady complains of colicky left iliac fossa pain. This is associated with distension and flatulence. On examination she is tender to palpation in the left iliac fossa and the sigmoid colon is palpable. Rectal examination is normal but stool samples are positive for occult blood. A barium enema is performed.

Figure 18

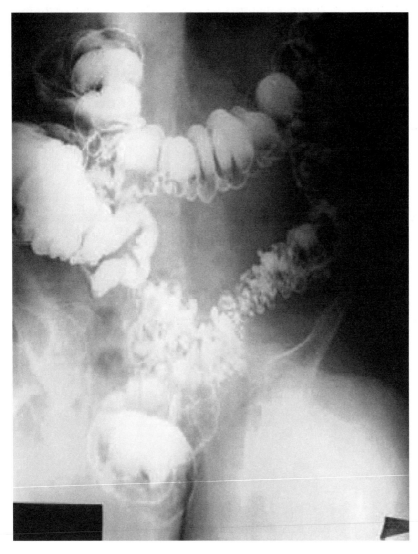

A   *What disease process does this barium enema show?*
B   *Should any further procedure be undertaken?*

Answer

A

The barium enema shows a narrowed segment of sigmoid colon with numerous outpouchings from the wall of the colon; these are **sigmoid diverticula**. There is also thickening of the transverse mucosal folds in the sigmoid colon due to smooth muscle hypertrophy. Although no other lesion was seen on the barium enema to account for the faecal occult blood, endoscopy of the segment of diverticular disease is needed. Other pathology within an area of diverticular disease can be obscured by the diverticular disease.

B

Complications of diverticular disease include progressive fibrosis leading to a fibrotic stricture which may present as a large bowel obstruction, haemorrhage which can be profuse and require blood transfusion or emergency surgery. Fistula formation into adjacent structures such as bladder, small bowel and vagina, may occur in a small number of cases.

Answer
overleaf

A 76-year-old man has delayed reporting difficulty with swallowing to his General Practitioner. He gives a four-month history of difficulty swallowing solids. More recently, however, this has progressed so that he is only able to swallow very soft food and fluids. He has lost 25 lb in weight.

On examination he has dry skin and there is evidence of weight loss. The GP also notices nicotine-stained fingers and the patient admits to a high alcohol intake in the past.

An urgent barium swallow is requested by the GP; following this the patient is referred to the thoracic surgeons for further management.

Figure 19

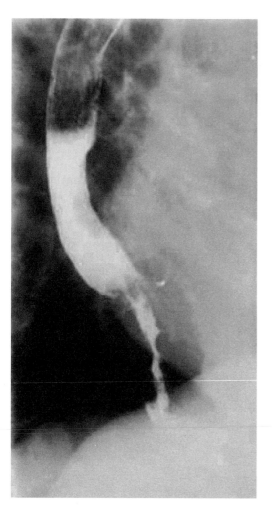

A   *What does the barium swallow show?*
B   *Why did he present late?*

Answer

A

The barium swallow shows a narrow segment of the distal third of the oesophagus. The margins are shouldered and there is loss of the normal smooth mucosa. The lumen is reduced to about 3 mm diameter. This has the appearance of a **carcinoma of the oesophagus**.

B

The major predisposing factors in the development of oesophageal carcinoma are smoking and a high alcohol intake. Patients often delay seeking advice. The tumours are often extensive by the time of presentation. The oesophagus is easily distensible and a tumour can reach a considerable size. Dysphagia only occurs when the tumour has encircled most of the circumference of the oesophageal wall. There is often distal spread.

Endoscopy should be carried out to obtain an histological diagnosis. Further radiological investigation is aimed at determining whether the lesion would be amenable to surgery. Ultrasound scanning of the liver to look for metastases and CT scanning is used to assess spread of tumour into adjacent structures and to look for distant lymph node metastases.

Answer
overleaf

A 27-year-old man complains of difficulty and pain on swallowing of recent onset. He has noticed some white spots on his hard palate which are not painful. A barium swallow is carried out.

Figure 20

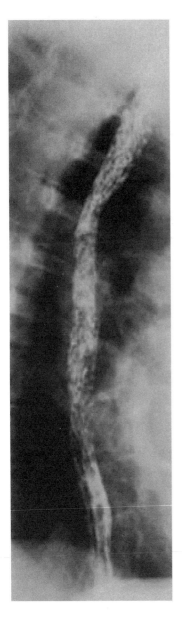

A   *What mucosal abnormality is seen?*
B   *What underlying process should be considered?*

Answer

A

The normal oesophageal mucosa should be smooth when coated and outlined with barium. In this case there is extensive nodularity of the whole of the oesophagus and along the margins there are small outpouchings of barium consistent with ulceration. During the examination, decreased oesophageal peristaltic activity may also be apparent.

B

This is an extensive ulcerative oesophagitis seen typically with infection by *Candida albicans*. Oesophageal ulceration may be seen with other infective agents such as herpes simplex virus. The ulceration is too extensive to be due to reflux oesophagitis. Other rarely encountered causes of oesophageal ulceration include Crohn's disease, tuberculosis, drugs and caustic ingestion.

Candida oesophagitis is seen mainly in immuno-compromised patients who may be receiving chemotherapy or radiotherapy. It may also be seen in association with HIV disease. It may also be seen in debilitated elderly patients.

A 58-year-old lady gives a history of tiredness, anorexia and loss of weight over several weeks. Her GP has checked her haemoglobin and a blood film shows mild iron deficiency anaemia. She is referred for a barium meal. No abnormality is seen in the oesophagus but a view of the stomach is shown.

Figure 21

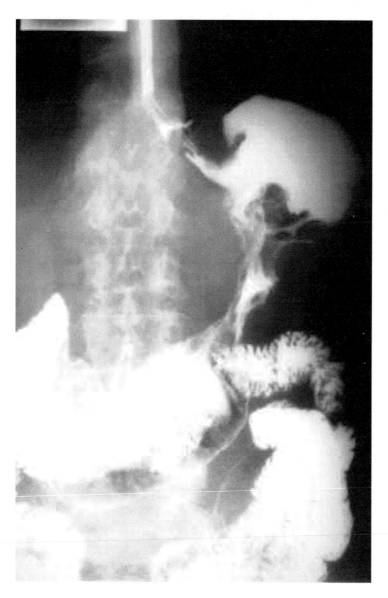

A   *What abnormality is seen?*

Answer

A

There is a large lesion extending along the lesser curve of the stomach and extending around to the greater curve. The normal rugal folds of the stomach are seen in the fundus and the gastric antrum shows a normal smooth mucosal pattern; the mucosal folds in between are distorted and destroyed. These appearances are those of a **large gastric carcinoma**.

Patients with carcinoma of the stomach often give a relatively long history of anorexia and feel tired. This is due to the anaemia that is present in about 45% of patients. Carcinoma of the stomach is frequently advanced by the time patients present with significant symptoms. The diagnosis should be confirmed by endoscopy with biopsy. As with oesophageal carcinoma, ultrasound and CT are valuable in assessing spread and in planning treatment. Although carcinoma is the most common tumour of the stomach, other tumours such as gastro-intestinal stromal tumours (eg leiomyoma), lymphoma and metastatic tumours may be encountered.

A 28-year-old man complains of repeated attacks of epigastric pain, usually occurring about two hours after food. He is often woken in the early morning by the same pain. He has a good appetite and has not lost any weight. He has found that attacks are often associated with stress at work. His GP had prescribed ranitidine but the patient has stopped taking them due to minor side-effects of occasional headaches. A barium meal is performed and a localised view of the duodenum is shown.

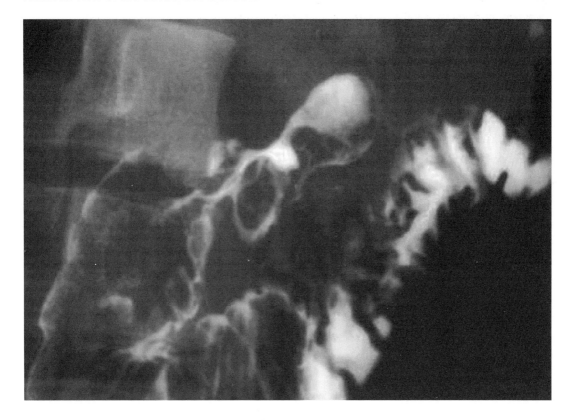

Figure 22

A   *What does it show?*

Answer

A

This is a film from a double contrast barium meal. The duodenum has been coated with barium and an effervescent agent producing CO_2. The first part of the duodenum, the duodenal cap has lost its normal triangular configuration and is distorted. Barium is collecting in a pool on the posterior aspect of the first part of the duodenum. This is a typical appearance of a **duodenal ulcer**.

In patients with duodenal ulceration unresponsive to conventional therapy, the choice of investigation is between a double contrast barium meal and endoscopy. Endoscopy usually requires intravenous sedation and usually a patient needs to take a day off work. A barium meal takes less time and does not require the administration of sedation. Most young patients now would have a trial of medical therapy and if symptoms fail to respond further investigation would be advised.

An obese 56-year-old lady complains of recurrent episodes of retrosternal pain which tends to occur when she goes to bed, often keeping her awake. Sometimes it radiates between her shoulder blades and occasionally down her left arm. It is usually relieved by sitting upright. Regurgitation of bitter fluid is also a problem at night. Occasionally she has a sensation of food sticking in the lower oesophagus.

On examination she is noted to be moderately obese and hypertensive. Because of her hypertension an electrocardiogram and chest radiograph are requested. The chest radiograph is shown.

Figure 23

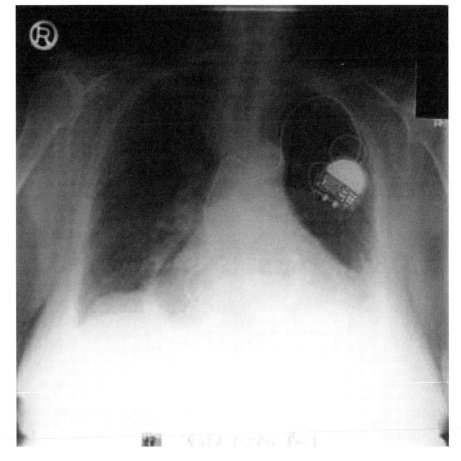

A   *What is the lucency seen through the heart shadow?*
B   *How can this be confirmed?*

Answer

A

The lucency seen through the heart shadow is air in a **hiatus hernia**. The fundus of the stomach has herniated through the oesophageal hiatus and the oesophago-gastric junction lies above the diaphragm. This is often seen as an incidental finding in elderly patients.

B

Confirmation of the hiatus hernia can be obtained either by a barium swallow or endoscopy. Barium swallow will allow an assessment of oesophageal motility and gastro-oesophageal reflux may be observed. Note also the single chamber pacing system.

Answer
overleaf

A 35-year-old male patient has been suffering with abdominal pain for two years. He has frequency of bowel motions for the past 15 months and in the last nine months has lost one stone in weight. He is admitted from casualty with increasing abdominal pain. His initial blood tests reveal a haemoglobin of 9.7 mmol/L and an albumin of 27 g/L.

His supine abdominal and erect chest X-rays appear normal. He appears stable over the next 48 hours.

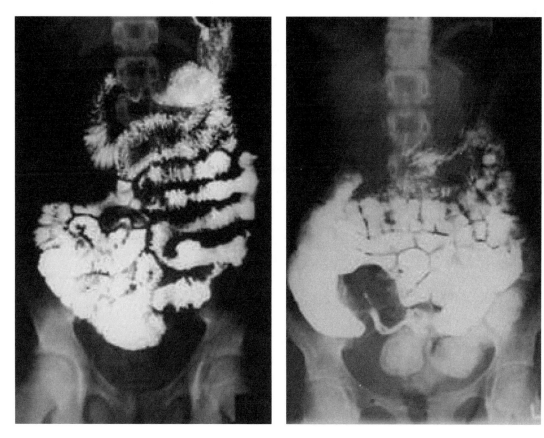

Figure 24a   **Figure 24b**

A   *What investigation should you request and how would it be performed?*
B   *What is the diagnosis?*

Answer

A

A small bowel meal should be requested to demonstrate the small bowel.
The patient must have fasted for a minimum of six hours so that food residue is not present.
Some centres advocate the use of laxatives to clear the large bowel and reduce transit time.
A suspension of barium sulphate is used. The liquid is quite viscous and has a chalky texture to it.

The patient is assessed to make sure there are no contra-indications to the procedure, eg large bowel obstruction, or bowel perforation. The patient is given a cupful of the mixture and the radiologist may screen with X-rays as the liquid enters the oesophagus and stomach. The patient is given further barium to drink until the whole small bowel and proximal large bowel have been visualised. The radiologist screens at regular intervals as this is a dynamic study and much information is gained by watching peristaltic movements.

The total amount of barium required varies between individuals but is usually 200-300 ml. The time taken for the study also varies and may be as little as one hour or as long as six hours. The patient should be warned of this.

This study demonstrates multiple irregular strictures (large arrows). These may be due to spasm, oedema or fibrosis and when the area is extremely narrow. The study also demonstrates ulceration, seen as outward projections (small arrows); separation of bowel wall loops which implies bowel wall oedema; and thickening from inflammation.

B

The diagnosis is **Crohn's disease** which nearly always affects the terminal ileum but can affect the anterior part of the GI tract, often leaving relatively normal bowel in between - the so-called skip lesions. Fine ulceration combined with mucosal oedema gives a cobblestone appearance. Fistulae may develop to other small bowel loops, large bowel, bladder or vagina.

The small bowel may also be demonstrated by a small bowel enema or enteroclysis study where a tube is passed through the nose into the stomach and advanced to the junction of the duodenum and jejunum. Contrast is then administered through the tube, producing better distension and demonstration of bowel folds.

Answer overleaf

A 32-year-old woman presents with a six-month history of loose bowel motions, often containing fresh blood. She has not seen a doctor previously as she is too afraid. She is seen in casualty where she is noted to be pale, tachycardic and is passing bright red blood per rectum. She is resuscitated and improves over the next 24 hours.

Figure 25

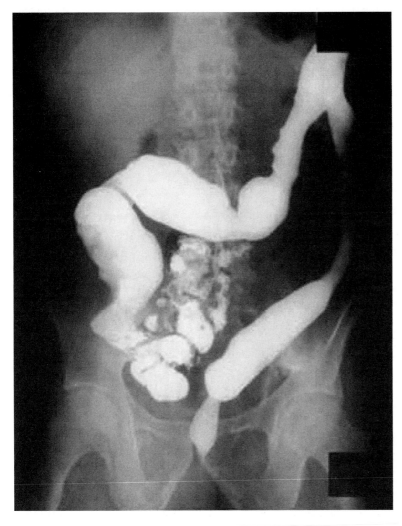

A   *What radiological investigation has been performed?*
B   *What is the diagnosis?*

Answer

A

This is a single contrast enema also known as a limited enema. Air is usually introduced into the bowel once barium has been administered and a double contrast effect is produced. However, if there is an increased risk of perforation a limited enema without bowel preparation and distension by air can be performed, eg for suspected large bowel obstruction or colitis. In the latter condition the bowel may be so friable or inflamed that distension with air may cause perforation.

The large bowel is featureless, ie the haustral pattern has been lost. This is because of marked inflammation within the bowel. This pattern may occur with any of the causes of colitis, for example:

■ inflammatory bowel disease, especially ulcerative colitis
■ infections, eg salmonella, shigella, ischaemic colitis
■ drug-induced, eg pseudomembranous colitis.

B

This patient has had an acute exacerbation of **ulcerative colitis**.

Chapter 2
CHEST

A 70-year-old smoker presents to his GP with a long history of increasing exertional breathlessness that is inhibiting his activities of daily living. On examination of the chest he has a hyper-expanded chest with hyper-resonant percussion and reduced breath sounds throughout. A chest X-ray is performed.

Figure 1

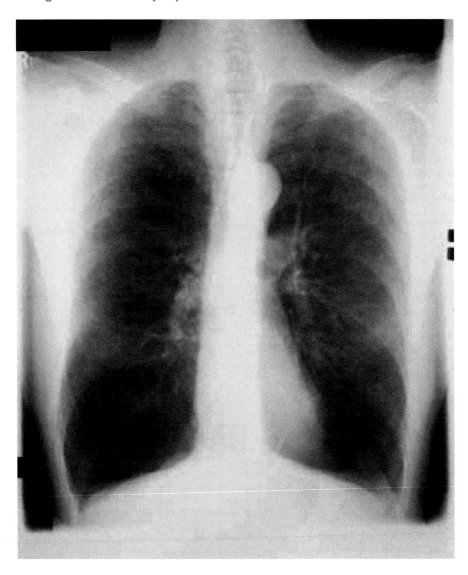

A   *Describe the chest X-ray abnormalities.*
B   *What is the most likely diagnosis?*

Answer

A

The lungs are hyper-expanded; 9 ribs are seen anteriorly instead of 6 and the hemidiaphragms are low and flat. There is attenuation of the blood vessels with a paucity of vessels at both bases.

B
Emphysema

Emphysema pathologically is a permanent enlargement of the air spaces distal to the terminal bronchioles with destruction of air space walls. This most commonly affects the upper lobes but in alpha-1 antitrypsin deficiency the lower lobes are more commonly affected. The chest X-ray is useful to make the diagnosis and to look for concurrent pathology such as neoplasm, infection or pneumothorax.

Answer overleaf

A 75-year-old gentleman presents to his GP with increasing exertional breathlessness. On examination he is breathless at rest, cyanosed and clubbed. Examination of the chest reveals fine inspiratory crackles at both bases. A chest X-ray was performed.

Figure 2

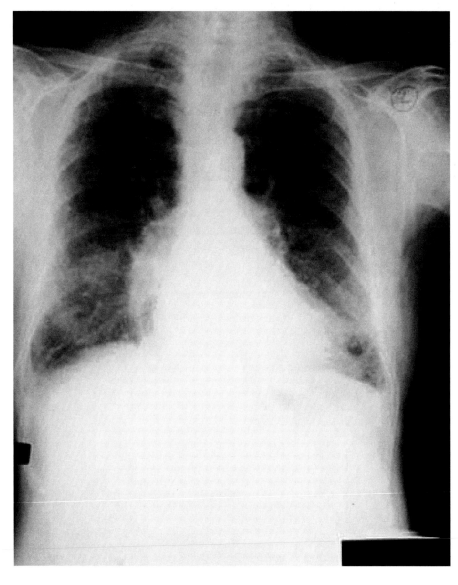

A   *Describe the chest X-ray abnormalities.*
B   *What is the most likely diagnosis?*

Answer

A

The lungs are of small volume. There are bilateral bibasal interstitial changes of fine lines and small nodules. There is loss of clarity of the left heart border. There is a 2 cm, well circumscribed lesion seen projected over the right lower zones.

B
Fibrosing alveolitis

Excluding masses and nodules there are two main patterns of lung shadowing: Air space shadowing and interstitial shadowing. Air space shadowing will be discussed later. Interstitial shadowing is due to abnormalities of the interstitium which is the connective tissue and lymphatics that support the airways. The pattern is characterised by fine lines and small nodules (reticular, nodular). If this pattern is suspected and it is often subtle, look for it at the periphery of the lung which should not have any structures present.

Common causes of interstitial disease are:

▌ Bilateral: Lung fibrosis; raised pulmonary venous pressure due to heart failure
▌ Unilateral: Lymphatic obstruction from tumour; lymphangitis carcinomatosa.

An important complication of fibrosis is the development of cancer and the mass in the right lung was proven to be a carcinoma on biopsy.

Answer
overleaf

A 65-year-old gentleman presents to his GP with haemoptysis, weight loss and recurrent fevers. There is a previous history of occupational asbestos exposure. A chest X-ray is performed.

Figure 3

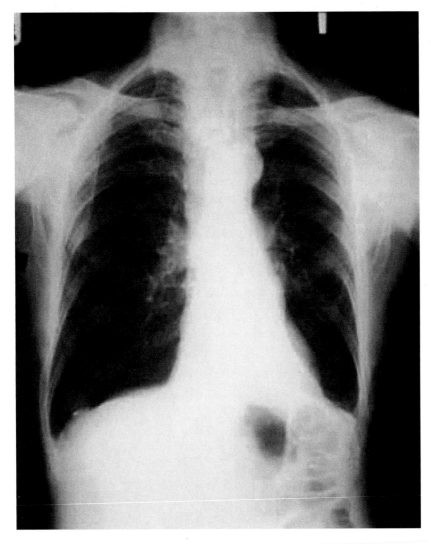

A   *Describe the chest X-ray abnormalities.*
B   *What is the most likely diagnosis?*

Answer

A

There is increased density behind the left heart with a soft tissue line extending behind the left heart down to the left hemidiaphragm. The left hilum is pulled downwards and the mediastinum is shifted towards the left. A calcific density is projected over the dome of the right hemidiaphragm.

B

Left lower lobe collapse, most likely due to an endobronchial lesion. The calcification represents pleural calcification from previous asbestos exposure.

Collapse/volume loss

The signs of collapse are the visualisation of the collapsed lobe (as in this case) and the effect it has on the surrounding lung and mediastinum. In this case the collapsed left lobe can be seen behind the heart and the left hilum is pulled down. There is hyperexpansion of the left upper lobe in compensation. Note the left lower lobe becomes solid and in compensation. Note the left lower lobe becomes solid so the silhouette sign of the left hemidiaphragm is lost.

Complications of asbestos exposure

▌ Mesothelioma
▌ Basal lung fibrosis
▌ Bronchogenic carcinoma

An 85-year-old gentleman presents to casualty in a state of circulatory collapse.
On examination he is pyrexial, very unwell with a blood pressure of 70/40 mmHg.
Examination of the chest reveals decreased expansion on the left side, dullness to percussion
and absent breath sounds. A supine chest radiograph is performed.

Figure 4

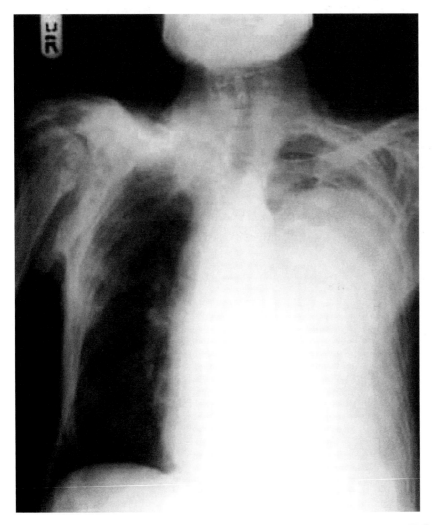

A *Describe the chest X-ray abnormalities.*
B *What further investigations should be performed?*

Answer

A

There is opacification of the left hemithorax with loss of the silhouette sign of the left heart border and left hemidiaphragm. A well defined upper margin can be seen, which is convex and the left apex is aerated. There is mass effect with pushing of the mediastinum towards the right. The bones are abnormal with expansion of the right humerus and coarsening of the primary trabecular pattern in keeping with a diagnosis of Paget's disease.

B

Pleural collection of fluid/pus should be suspected so ultrasound guided chest drain should be inserted and a sample sent for microscopy, culture and sensitivity and tuberculous culture.

A 35-year-old male presents to casualty with sudden onset of shortness of breath. On examination he was breathless at rest, centrally cyanosed with a systolic blood pressure of 100 mmHg. Examination of the chest revealed decreased expansion on the left side with absent breath sounds and hyper-resonance to percussion. The trachea and apex beat were shifted towards the right.

Figure 5

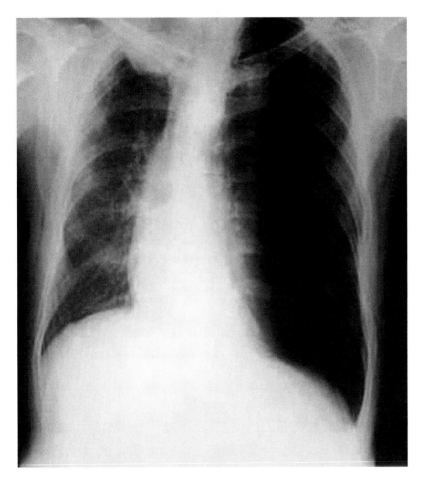

A   *What diagnosis should be suspected on clinical findings?*
B   *What emergency procedure should be performed?*

Answer

A & B

On clinical findings a tension pneumothorax should be suspected and large gauge needle inserted into the left chest to release the air under tension (**before** requesting a chest X-ray).

The chest X-ray of this gentleman revealed a tension pneumothorax with absent vascular markings in the periphery of the left lung, a clear lung edge seen and the mediastinum shifted towards the right.

A 55-year-old female smoker presents to her GP with pain in the right arm and cough. Examination of the patient reveals a right-sided Horner's lesion. On examination of the chest there is dullness to percussion over the right clavicle and absent breath sounds at the apex. A chest X-ray is performed.

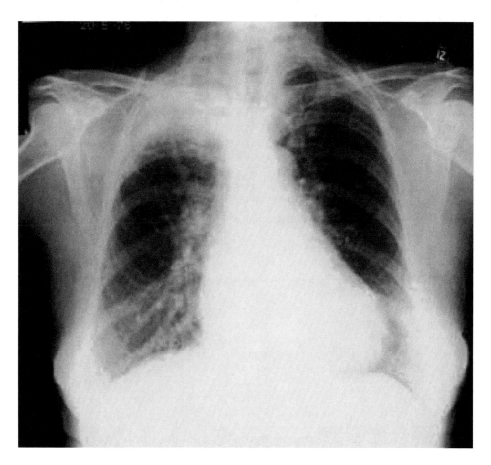

Figure 6

A   *Describe the chest X-ray abnormalities.*
B   *What is the most likely diagnosis?*

Answer

A

There is soft tissue opacification of the right apex with no volume loss. The lateral aspect of the second rib is destroyed.

B

Bronchogenic carcinoma, **Pancoast's tumour**. Abnormal soft tissue at the apex is commonly seen with TB infection. It is the history and presence of rib destruction that gives the diagnosis of Pancoast's tumour.

A 40-year-old man presented to Casualty with a history of productive cough, temperature and anorexia. On examination, he is unwell with increased respiratory rate. There is decreased expansion of the chest on the left and bronchial breathing and dullness to percussion on the left side. A chest X-ray is performed.

Figure 7

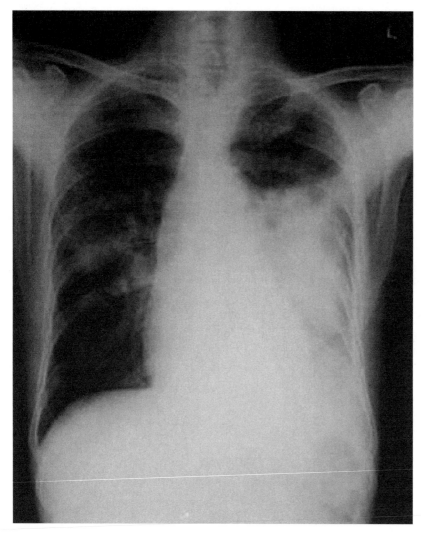

A *Describe the chest X-ray abnormalities.*
B *What is the most likely diagnosis?*

Answer

A

There is confluent shadowing in the left mid-zone, with lucencies consistent with air bronchogram. Note there is loss of silhouette of the left hemidiaphragm. This indicates solid lung is adjacent to the left hemidiaphragm 'loss of the silhouette sign'. Air bronchograms are pathognomonic of air space shadowing.

B

In view of the history and distribution of the consolidation this is consistent with **pneumonia**. Loss of the left hemidiaphragm and preservation of the left heart border indicate the pneumonia is in the left lower lobe.

Air space shadowing

Air space shadowing in the right middle lobe. Loss of the right heart border and preservation of the silhouette of the right hemidiaphragm.

This is an example of the second pattern of lung shadowing 'air space shadowing'. This is characterised by homogenous opacification and air bronchograms. The pathology is fluid within the air spaces which may be infectious, eg pneumonia, oedematous fluid, eg heart failure, adult respiratory distress syndrome or haemorrhage.

Air bronchograms are air in bronchi surrounded by solid lung. The lung becomes solid and, therefore, when it is adjacent to a solid organ the air to soft tissue interface is lost so there is loss of the silhouette sign.

Answer overleaf

A 60-year-old smoker presents to casualty with increasing breathlessness over a period of time and weight loss. Examination of the chest reveals decreased expansion on the right side, stony dullness to percussion and absent breath sounds. A chest radiograph is performed.

Figure 8

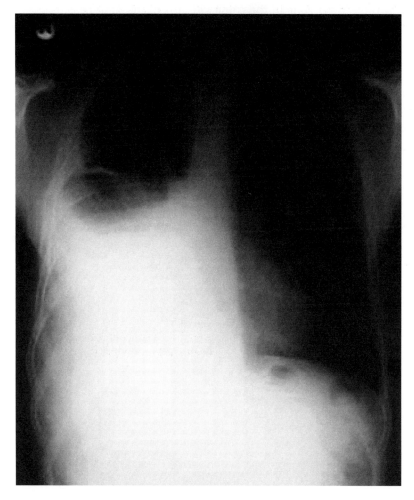

A *Describe the chest X-ray abnormalities.*
B *What is the most likely diagnosis?*

Answer

A

There is opacification of the right lower zone of the chest with loss of the right heart border and right hemidiaphragm. A meniscus is seen lateral and superior to the opacification which would be in keeping with a pleural effusion.

B

A **unilateral pleural effusion** is most likely to be an exudate. Malignancy and infection are the most common causes. Aspiration/drainage is recommended and a sample should be sent for cytology and microbiology. Transudate effusions have a low protein content and are due to systemic illness such as heart and renal failure, so they are usually bilateral. Exudate effusions have a high protein content and are due to local lung/pleural disease, so they are unilateral.

A 65-year-old female presents to casualty with a short history of severe interscapular chest pain. On examination she has different blood pressures in each arm and there is dullness to percussion and absent breath sounds in the left lower chest.

Figure 9

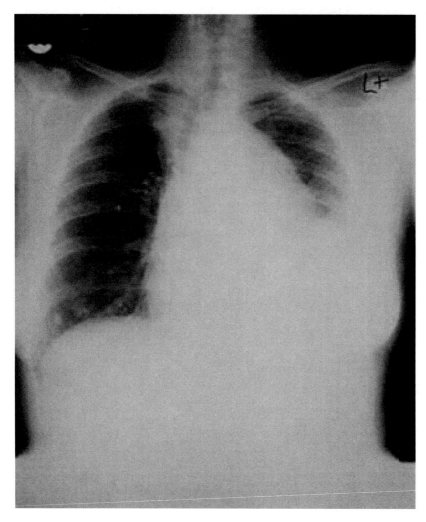

A   Describe the chest X-ray abnormalities.
B   What is the most likely diagnosis?

Answer

A

There is widening of the upper mediastinum. There is loss of clarity of the aortic arch which appears to be expanded. There is loss of the left hemidiaphragm and left heart border due to soft tissue opacity which is most likely due to fluid.

B

The most likely diagnosis is **aortic dissection** which is due to spontaneous longitudinal separation of the media of the aortic wall produced by haemorrhage. Contrast enhanced helical CT is important to confirm the diagnosis and demonstrate the extent of dissections. Aortic dissections distal to the arch of the aorta are managed medically, dissections involving the origin and aortic arch are considered for surgery.

NB: Blood can dissect down into the pericardial sac and cause tamponade.

A 30-year-old Asian gentleman presented to his GP with a history of night sweats, weight loss and productive cough. A chest X-ray was performed.

Figure 10

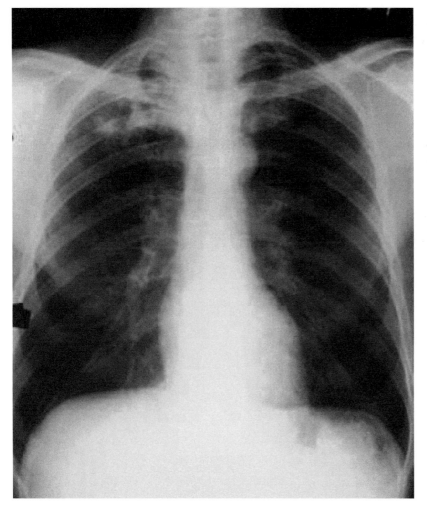

A *Describe the chest X-ray abnormalities.*
B *What is the most likely diagnosis?*
C *What is the management?*

Answer

A
Air space shadowing is seen in the right apex with cavitation. No other focal lung lesion is seen. The mediastinum appears normal.

B
The most likely diagnosis is **pulmonary tuberculosis**. Cavitating lung lesions are commonly caused by infection, malignancy and infarction. Bacterial infections Staph. aureus and Klebsiella commonly contribute as does mycobacteria. The most common tumour to cavitate is a primary bronchogenic squamous cell carcinoma.

C
The patient needs urgent referral to the chest clinic. In some hospitals this referral is made by the radiologist when the film is reported to prevent delay in starting treatment.

A 60-year-old man with a known past history of ischaemic heart disease presents to the Accident and Emergency department with a short history of increasing breathlessness. On examination the patient is breathless, has a raised jugular venous pressure and ankle swelling.

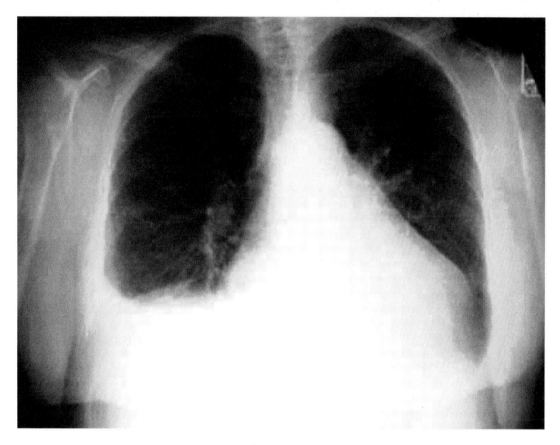

Figure 11

A   *Describe the X-ray abnormalities.*
B   *What is the diagnosis?*

Answer

A

The heart is enlarged with enlargement of the upper lobe vessels when compared to the lower lobe vessels, ie a redistribution of blood. This is in keeping with a raised left atrial pressure from left heart dysfunction. Bilateral pleural effusions are also seen. Kerley B lines are seen bilaterally (these are small interstitial lines that extend at the bases horizontally and peripherally). There is no evidence of pulmonary oedema.

B

The diagnosis is **congestive cardiac failure**.

Answer overleaf

A 30-year-old asthmatic male presents to his GP with a short history of increased exertional breathlessness.

On examination the signs are limited to the right hemithorax with decreased expansion, decreased breath sounds and hyper-resonance. The apex of the heart and trachea are not shifted. The patient is referred to hospital for X-ray.

Figure 12

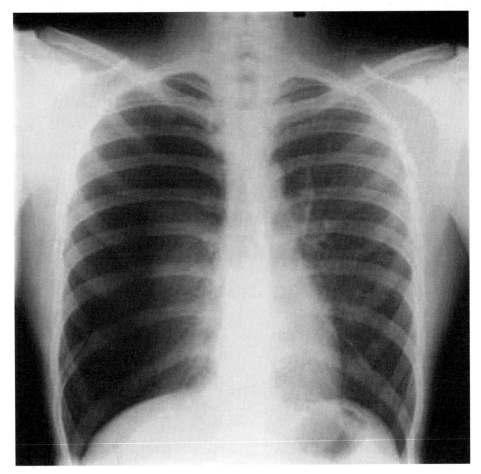

A   Describe the X-ray abnormality.
B   What is the diagnosis and further management?

Answer

A
There is absence of lung markings in the periphery of the right hemithorax. A lung edge can be seen.

B
The diagnosis is a **pneumothorax**. Importantly there is no mediastinal shift to the left indicating the absence of tension. As the patient is symptomatic he should be referred to the Accident and Emergency department for aspiration of the air in the pleural cavity or insertion of chest drain.

Chapter 3
BONES

Answer
overleaf

A 45-year-old Asian woman presents with generalised pain and weakness in her pelvis and legs.

Figure 1a

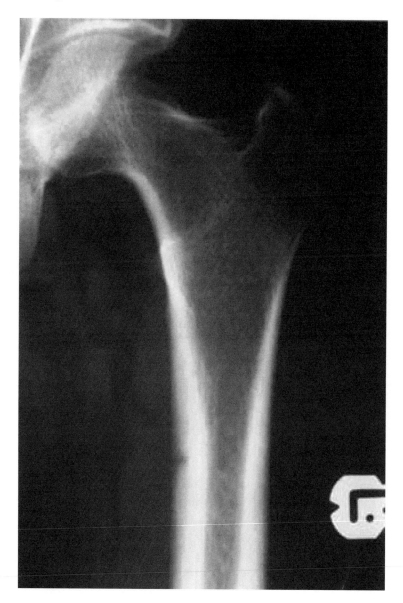

This is the X-ray of her right femur.

A   *What is the radiographic abnormality?*
B   *What is the diagnosis?*

Answer

A

There is a lucency in the medial aspect of the cortex which is characteristic of a **Looser's zone.** This is an insufficiency fracture that does not unite. The fracture is due to normal stresses but these occur on abnormal bone. The bone is abnormal because there is insufficient mineralisation due to disturbance of calcium and phosphate caused by vitamin D deficiency.

Figure 1b

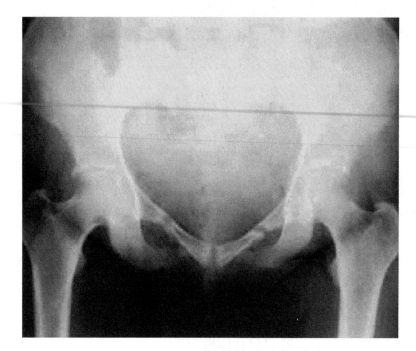

B

Looser's zones are also commonly found in the pubic rami. The pelvic X-ray (Fig 1b) from a different patient demonstrates these. Looser's zones are the diagnostic radiological features of osteomalacia. Reduction in bone density is also a feature, but it is not specific.

The bone disorder caused by vitamin D deficiency is known as osteomalacia in adults and rickets in children. Rickets also has other causes (see case 5, page 91).

Answer overleaf

A 30-year- old patient presents with nausea and vomiting. Her serum calcium is 3.8 mmol/L and her phosphate is 0.5 mmol/L. The alkaline phosphatase is 300 U/L.

Figure 2a

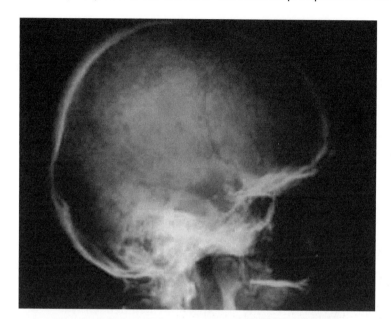

Figure 2b

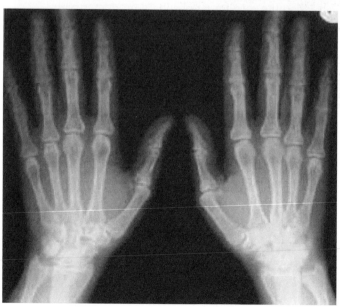

A *What is the likely diagnosis?*
B *What do the X-rays show and why?*
C *What other symptoms may be produced by this condition?*

Answer

A

The likely diagnosis is **hyperparathyroidism.** Parathyroid hormone maintains the level of calcium in the blood by promoting osteoclastic activity. (Osteoblastic activity is also increased, but much less so than the osteoclastic activity.) This causes breakdown/resorption of bone and calcium is freed from bone into the blood.

B
Skull
There are multiple small lucencies in the skull giving a 'pepperpot skull'. The lesions are smaller and less well defined than in multiple myeloma (see Case 3, page 85).

Hands
There is subperiosteal bone resorption involving the phalangeal tufts and radial aspect of the middle phalanges.

C

In addition to bone resorption, bone softening also occurs. Brown tumours may develop which are focal areas of increased osteoclastic activity and appear as well defined lytic lesions. Soft tissue calcification occurs when the calcium x phosphate product is high. Erosive arthropathy may also occur; this simulates rheumatoid arthritis but the joint space is preserved.

A raised serum calcium causes:
▮ nausea and vomiting
▮ renal calculi
▮ peptic ulcer disease
▮ pancreatitis.

A 32-year-old Asian man presents with a three-week history of back pain. In the last few days he has had progressive weakness of his legs.

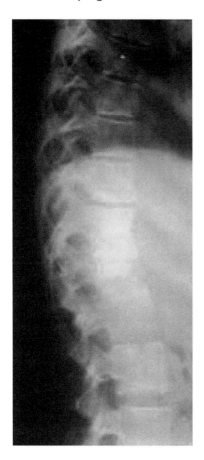

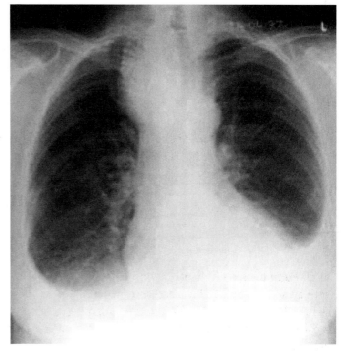

Figure 3b

Figure 3a

A   *What do his X-rays show?*
B   *What is the diagnosis?*

Answer

A

There is an abnormality of T12 and L1 and the T12/L1 intervertebral disc. There is marked loss of alignment of these two vertebrae. The chest X-ray shows a cavitating apical lesion on the right in keeping with **tuberculosis**.

B

The most likely cause of this appearance is an infection of the disc (discitis) with spread of the infection into the adjoining vertebral bodies. A tumour/metastatic deposit rarely crosses the disc space so involvement of the disc makes the diagnosis infection until proven otherwise.

Tuberculosis should be considered, but other organisms, eg *Staph. aureus* can also be responsible.

A 57-year-old man presents with painful wrists and ankles. On examination his wrists and ankles are extremely tender and swollen. He also has a cough which he admits to having for over three months.

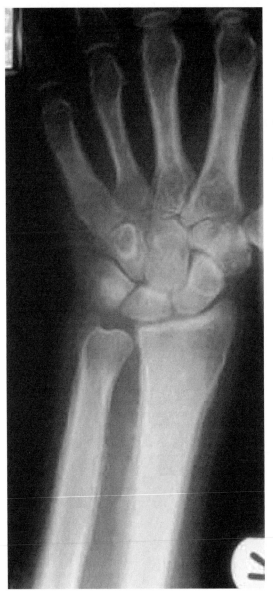

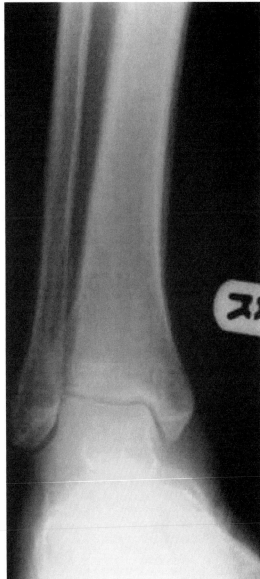

Figure 4ai   **Figure 4aii**

A(i) *What do his wrist and leg X-rays show?*
A(ii) *What is your management?*

Answer

4a(i) and 4a(ii)

There is an undulating periosteal reaction in the distal radius and ulnar and distal femur. The appearances are in keeping with **hypertrophic osteoarthropathy** (HOA). The most likely cause is a primary bronchial neoplasm and a chest X-ray should be performed.

Figure 4b

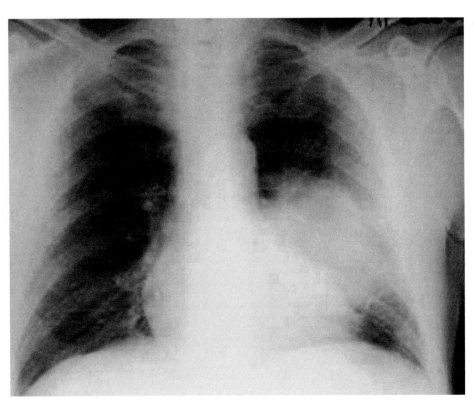

B(i)   *This is the same patient's chest X-ray. What does it show?*
B(ii) *What are other possible causes of HOA?*

Answer

B(i)
The chest X-ray shows a large left mid-zone mass in keeping with a bronchial carcinoma.

B(ii)
Other thoracic causes of HOA include:
- mesothelioma
- lymphoma,
- chronic infection, eg abscess
- bronchiectasis
- cystic fibrosis
- interstitial fibrosis
- pleural fibroma
- thymoma
- rib tumours
- congenital cyst.

Extrathoracic causes include:
- ulcerative colitis
- Crohn's disease
- bowel lymphoma
- Whipple's disease
- cirrhosis
- liver abscess
- pancreatic carcinoma.

Answer
overleaf

An 18-month-old Asian boy is taken to his GP by his parents who are concerned that he is unable to stand unsupported. On examination he is small, has slight bowing of his tibia and is unable to weight-bear. His wrists and ankles are swollen and his dentition is delayed.

The GP is concerned about the boy's condition and requests an X-ray of his knees and refers him to the local paediatrician.

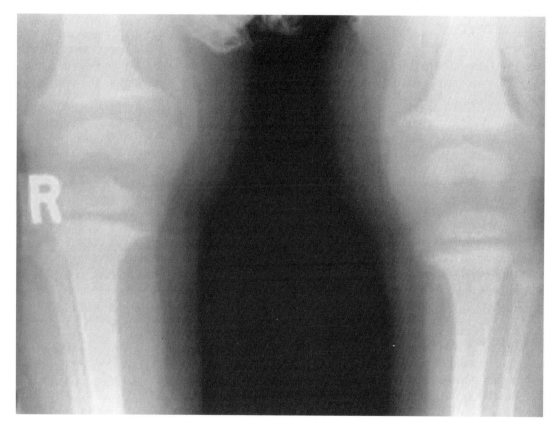

Figure 5

A *What does the X-ray show?*
B *What is the diagnosis?*
C *What are some possible causes?*

Answer

A

There is irregularity of the metaphyses with splaying and cupping.

B

These are important radiographic features of **rickets.**

C

The metaphyses of the long bones which are subjected to stress are particularly affected, eg wrists, ankles and knees. In addition there is widening of the epiphyseal plate and delayed appearance of the epiphyses. There is demineralisation of the bones.

Rickets usually occurs between four and 18 months. Patients present with irritability, bone pain and tenderness. Softening of the bones produces bowing of the legs. Frontal bossing may also occur.

Causes of rickets

Abnormal vitamin D metabolism
1 **Vitamin D deficiency:** Lack of sunshine, poor dietary intake, malabsorption.
2 **Defective conversion of vitamin D to 25 OH cholecalciferol in the liver:** Liver disease, anti-convulsants.
3 **Defective conversion of 25 OH cholecalciferol to 1,25 OH cholecalciferol in the kidney:** Chronic renal failure, vitamin D-dependent rickets (autosomal recessive defect of 1 OH ase).

Abnormal phosphate metabolism
1 Poor intake, malabsorption.
2 Defective phosphate reabsorption by the kidney, eg renal tubular acidosis and primary hypophosphataemia (the latter is also known as vitamin D-resistant rickets).

Calcium deficiency
1 Dietary (rare), malabsorption.

A 79-year-old lady presents to her GP with pain in her joints. Her back, wrists, hips and knees are all affected. The pain is worse at the end of the day. Her full blood count and ESR are normal. Her GP arranges for some X-rays.

Figure 6

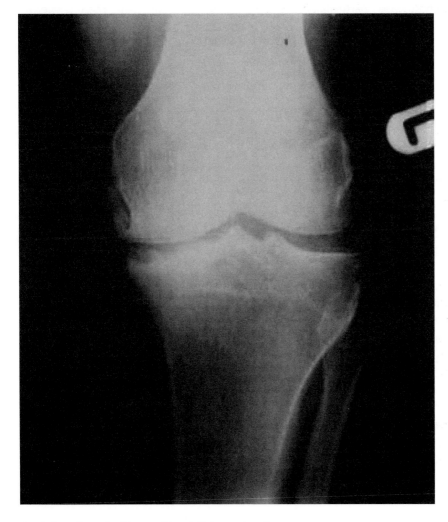

A   *What does the X-ray of her left knee show?*
B   *What is the diagnosis?*
C   *Which other joints are affected by this disease process?*

Answer

A

There is joint space narrowing, particularly of the medial joint compartment. There is sclerosis of the subchondral bone of the medial aspect of the tibia and subchondral cysts in the lateral aspect of the tibia. There are osteophytes projecting from the medial aspect of the femur and tibia.

B

These are the radiological signs of **osteoarthritis**.

C

In general the radiological signs are:
- joint space narrowing, especially in the weight-bearing area (medial compartment of the knee)
- sclerosis in areas of stress
- subchondral cyst formation (geodes)
- osteophytosis at the articular margin/non stressed area.

In the knee the medial compartment is most affected. In the hand and foot the first MCP and MTP joints are most affected. The first carpometacarpal is also affected. Osteophytes at the distal interphalangeal joint produce Heberden's nodes and at the proximal interphalangeal joints they produce Bouchard's nodes.

The pathogenesis is degeneration of the articular cartilage, which increases with age, abnormal pressure on the joints, eg obesity, dysplastic joint. Osteoarthritis also occurs in previously damaged joints, eg due to infection or trauma. It occurs in women 10 times more often than in men.

A 45-year-old female patient presents to her GP with morning stiffness, fatigue and weight loss. Her haemoglobin is 9.5 mmol/L and her ESR is 75 mm/hr.

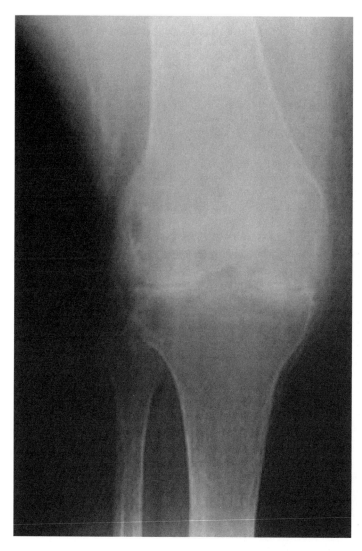

Figure 7

A   *What does her knee X-ray show?*
B   *What is the diagnosis?*

Answer

A
There is osteopenia (bone demineralisation) and symmetric loss of joint space.

B
The diagnosis is **rheumatoid arthritis**. Rheumatoid arthritis is a generalised connective tissue disease. The highest incidence is in the 4th and 5th decade. The male to female ratio is 1:3 under the age of 40 and 1:1 over 40.

The affected joints are tender and swollen. In the initial stages the excess intra-articular inflammatory tissue, which is the cause of the disease, can produce joint space widening. Later, the destruction by the inflammatory process, produces joint destruction and joint space narrowing.

There are many extra-articular manifestations of rheumatoid arthritis:

- **Pulmonary manifestations:** Pleural effusion, lung fibrosis, nodules, Caplan's syndrome, pulmonary hypertension.
- **Cardiovascular involvement:** Pericarditis, myocarditis.
- **Neurological sequelae:** Nerve entrapment (atlantoaxial subluxation, carpal tunnel syndrome).
- **Sjögren's syndrome:** Rheumatoid arthritis and keratoconjunctivitis and xerostomia.
- **Felty's syndrome:** Rheumatoid arthritis and splenomegaly and neutropenia.
- **Lymphadenopathy**

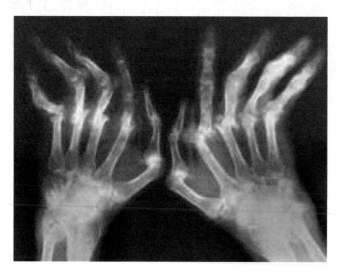

Figure 7b

Classically rheumatoid arthritis affects small joints of the wrist and hand in a symmetrical pattern.

Answer overleaf

A 65-year-old man presents to his GP complaining of fatigue and lower back pain. The GP checks the full blood count, urea and electrolytes calcium and phosphate and liver function tests. The blood tests come back as normal, apart from a markedly raised alkaline phosphatase. The GP requests a lumbar spine and pelvic X-ray.

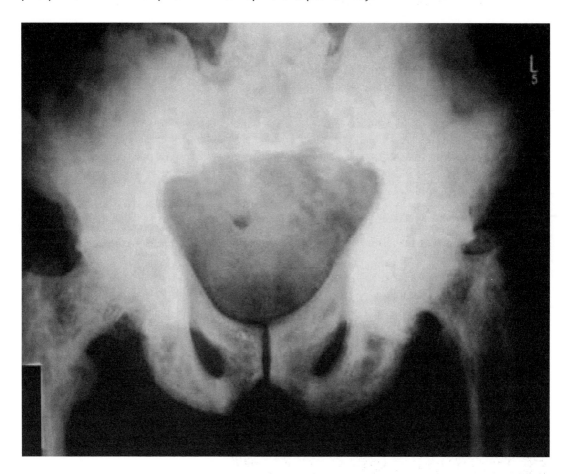

Figure 8

A   *What does the pelvic X-ray show?*
B   *What is the diagnosis?*
C   *What are the complications of this condition?*

Answer

A

The bone trabeculae are thick and coarse and there is cortical thickening, causing expansion of the pelvic bones.

B

The diagnosis is **Paget's disease**. Any bone can be affected by Paget's disease, but the skull, pelvis, long bones and spine are most commonly affected.

The disease affects 10% of people over 80. It is twice as common in men as in women. During the active phase of Paget's there is marked bone resorption and the X-ray appearance is of a lytic lesion. In the skull this is known as osteoporosis circumscripta. During the inactive phase there is decreased bone turnover with skeletal sclerosis. Usually there is a combination of the lytic and sclerotic phase.

C

In one fifth of patients the disease is asymptomatic. Some patients present with an enlarging hat size!

Peripheral nerve compression and hearing loss/blindness due to narrowing of the cranial nerve foramina, are also features. Pain due to the primary disease is unusual and suggests a pathological fracture, malignant transformation (rare) or degenerative joint disease.

High output cardiac failure from markedly increased perfusion can rarely occur. Local hyperthermia may sometimes occur.

A 20-year-old man presented to his GP with a long history of right shoulder pain which had been treated with physiotherapy as a frozen shoulder and increasing shortness of breath. On examination the signs of a right-sided pleural effusion were found. A chest X-ray was requested.

Figure 9

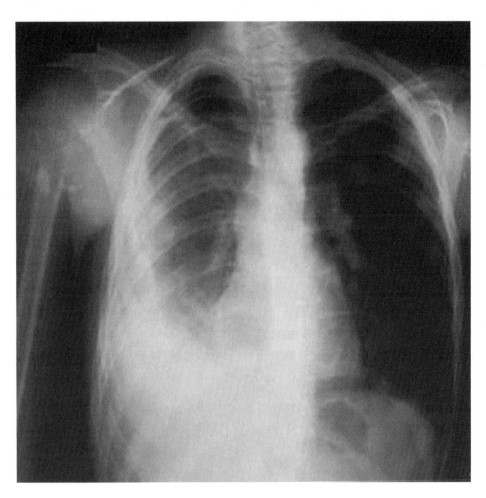

A   *Describe the abnormality of the right shoulder.*
B   *Describe the abnormality of the chest.*
C   *What is the unifying diagnosis?*

Answer

A
There is an abnormal tissue mass surrounding the metaphysis of the right humerus. The underlying bone is destroyed with lucencies and destruction of the cortex. There is lifting of the periosteum inferiorly consistent with Codman's triangle.

B
There is quite an extensive right-sided pleural effusion with multiple soft tissue opacities seen projected over the left lung.

C
In a patient of this age the most likely diagnosis is a **primary bone tumour** of the left shoulder, such as osteogenic sarcoma with metastatic deposits to the lungs. Osteogenic sarcoma is also known as an osteosarcoma. The lung metastases are often bone forming and therefore very dense.

An 86-year-old gentleman presents to casualty with non-specific abdominal pain. He had a long history of back pain and back stiffness. An abdominal X-ray was taken.

Figure 10

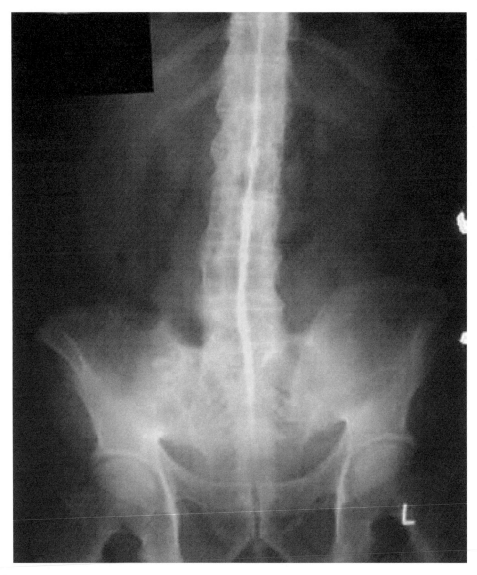

A   *Describe the abnormalities of the lumbar sacral spine.*
B   *What is the diagnosis?*
C   *Name three complications of this disorder.*

Answer

A

(a) The sacro-iliac joints cannot be seen as they have fused.

(b) There is ossification of the lateral aspect of the discs (annulus fibrosis) producing bridge osteophytes between vertebral bodies at multiple levels. These are termed syndesmophytes. The bridging syndesmophytes cause the spine to become fused and rigid also known as 'bamboo spine'.

(c) There is also mid-line calcification which is due to ossification of the anterior longitudinal ligaments.

B

The description of the lumbar spine with the appearance of a 'bamboo spine' and the fusion of the sacro-iliac joints would be consistent with **ankylosing spondylitis.**

C

Upper lobe pulmonary fibrosis, aortic incompetence and amyloid are all recognised complications of this disorder.

A 50-year-old diabetic patient with unknown peripheral vascular disease presented to the diabetic foot clinic with signs of an ischaemic toe and infection. A plain film was taken.

Figure 11

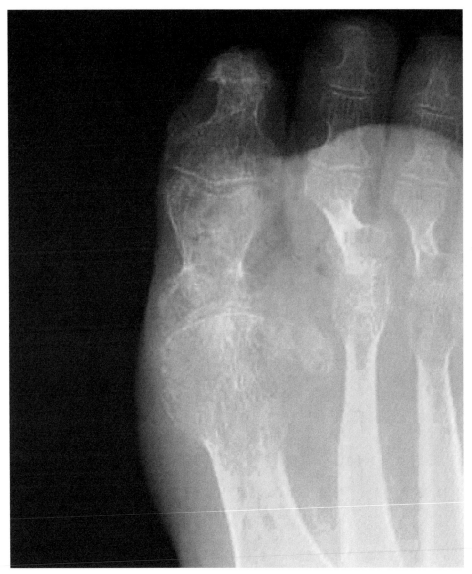

A *Describe the soft tissue abnormalities.*
B *What is the diagnosis?*

Answer

A

There are multiple lucencies in the soft tissue around the proximal and distal phalanx of the big toe. These lucencies represent gas.

B

Infection with gas producing organisms (eg *Clostridium perfringens*) is in keeping with a diagnosis of **gas gangrene**.

Chapter 4
NEUROLOGY

Answer
overleaf

1 A 50-year-old man presents to casualty with a history of sudden onset severe occipital headache and collapse. An urgent CT head is performed without contrast enhancement.

Figure 1

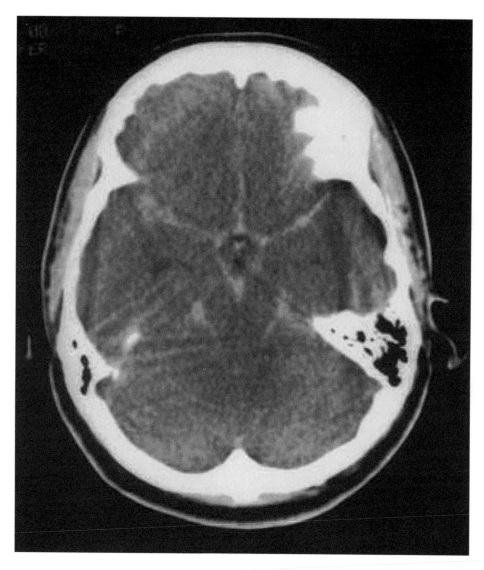

A *Describe the abnormalities on the CT.*
B *What is the diagnosis?*
C *What is the most likely cause?*
D *What further investigation is required?*

Answer

A

High attenuation material is seen within the basal cisterns of the brain. High attenuation material on a CT scan is due to haemorrhage, calcification or contrast medium. On an un-enhanced scan contrast medium has not been given and so calcium or haemorrhage are the causes. Calcification tends to occur in small focal areas and is of very high density. The appearance in this case is due to haemorrhage.

Haemorrhage may occur within various layers of the brain. It is extradural when it lies between the skull and the dural covering of the brain. It is subdural when it lies under the dura but above the brain. Both of these types of haemorrhage are intracranial, but extracerebral.

The subarachnoid space is the space between the arachnoid and the pia. The pia is the innermost meningeal layer and is closely applied to the brain. The subarachnoid space contains CSF and the major blood vessels. If one of these vessels ruptures this will produce a subarachnoid haemorrhage, with diffuse blood in the CSF containing space, eg the basal cisterns.

An intracerebral bleed occurs within the brain substance itself.

B

Diagnosis is a **subarachnoid haemorrhage.** Note that approximately 1% of patients with a subarachnoid haemorrhage will have a normal CT and to make the diagnosis a lumbar puncture needs to be performed to look for blood in the CSF.

C

An aneurysm of the circle of Willis is the most likely cause. Other causes include trauma, AV malformations.

D

Cerebral angiography is required to define the bleeding point.

Answer overleaf

A 70-year-old lady presents to casualty with right sided weakness. There is a history of trauma to the head 24 hours previously. An urgent CT head is performed.

Figure 2a

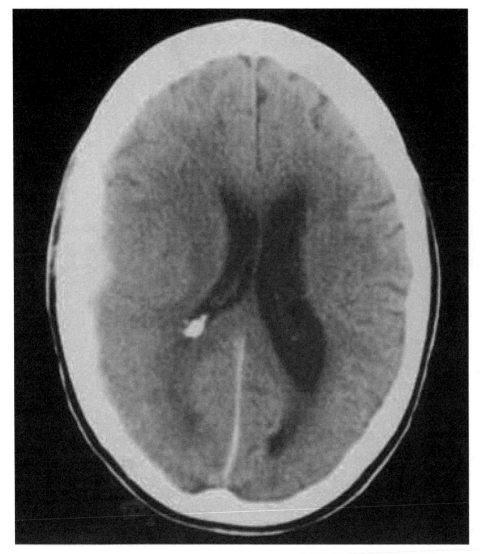

A   *Describe the CT abnormalities.*
B   *What is the diagnosis?*
C   *What further course of action should be taken?*
D   *What other chronic disease is the patient suffering from?*

Answer

A

There is an ellipsoid of high attenuation material in the right subdural space. This is having mass effect and causing compression of the ipsilateral lateral ventricle.

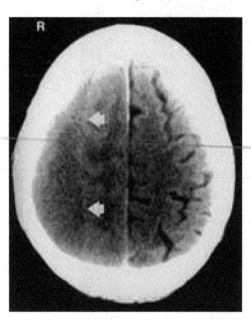

Figure 2b

B
Acute subdural haemorrhage

Subdural haematomas originate from bridging veins that cross the subdural space and subarachnoid space that connect the dural sinuses to the cerebral cortex. This space is enlarged in infants and the elderly and people with cerebral atrophy such as alcoholics. A shearing force across the veins from movement of the brain causes rupture and haemorrhage; because the haemorrhage is venous and low pressure, these haematomas may present insidiously over time. This is acute as the blood is of high attenuation. Blood which is two weeks old is isodense with brain see (answer A), as it becomes older than two weeks the attenuation decreases. Subdural haematomas that are isodense with brain can be difficult to detect. Unlike extradural haemorrhage there is no consistent relationship to skull fractures.

C
An urgent neurosurgical referral.

D

There is expansion of the bones of the skull in keeping with Paget's disease.

Answer
overleaf

A 30-year-old gentleman is brought into casualty after a high-speed road traffic accident; he has sustained trauma to the head only and has a reduced level of consciousness. An urgent CT scan of the head is performed.

Figure 3

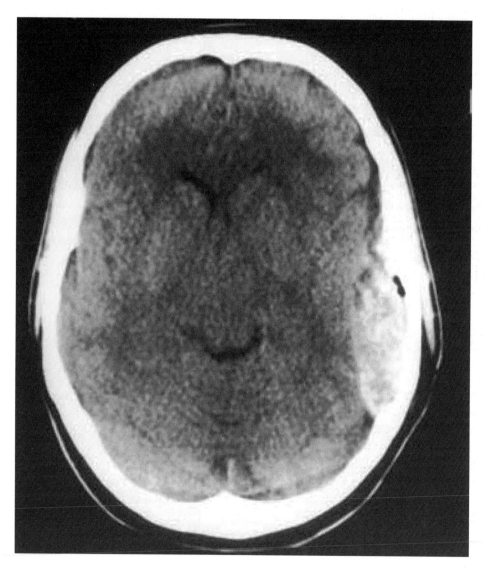

A *Describe the CT for abnormalities.*
B *What is the diagnosis?*
C *What further course of action should be taken?*

Answer

A

A convex area of high attenuation material is seen to extend from inner table of the skull on the left. This is causing mass effect with midline shift. A very small low attenuating area is seen in the peripheral to this.

B

Extradural haemorrhage with air within the skull vault in keeping with a skull fracture.
Extradural blood originates from arteries which are in close proximity to bone such as the middle meningeal artery. These arteries rupture with skull fracture and a rapidly enlarging haematoma occurs so the neurological symptoms occur soon after the trauma.
NB: Extradurals are convex with relation to the skull; subdurals are concave with relation to the skull.

C

Urgent neurosurgical referral.

Answer overleaf

A 55-year-old gentleman who is hypertensive presents to casualty with a sudden onset of reduced level of consciousness. An urgent CT scan of the head is performed.

Figure 4

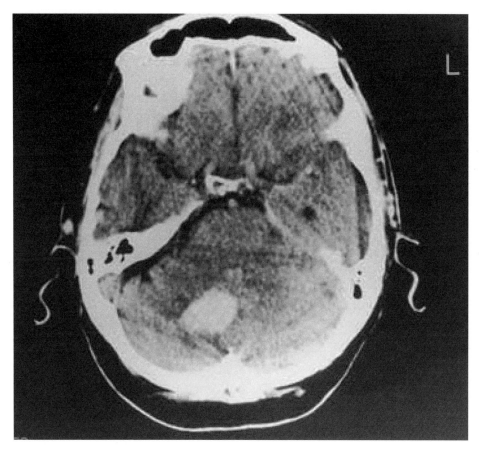

A   What is the indication for a CT head in this clinical?
B   Describe the CT and abnormalities.
C   What is the diagnosis?
D   What is the course of action?

Answer

A
A CT scan of the head is indicated in the unconscious patient to exclude a neurosurgical cause for the reduced level of consciousness.

B
High attenuation material consistent with fresh blood is seen within the right cerebellar hemisphere producing mass effect and compressing the 4th ventricle.

C
Primary intracerebral haemorrhage. This type of haemorrhage usually originates as a consequence of chronic hypertension from a ruptured small artery. Peripheral small aneurysms or atriovenous malformation may also present this way.

D
Urgent neurosurgical referral for consideration of evacuation of the haematoma.

Answer
overleaf

A 60-year-old lady presents to her GP with a short history of severe headaches which are worse in the morning and associated with nausea. She has a past history of breast carcinoma. She was referred for a contrast enhanced CT of the head.

Figure 5

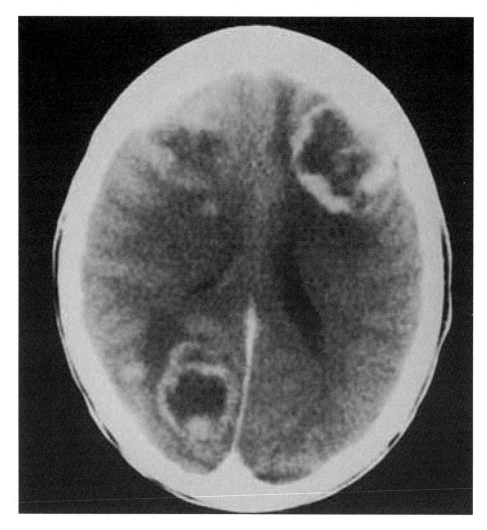

A   *Describe the CT and abnormalities.*
B   *What is the most likely diagnosis?*
C   *What is the next course of action?*

Answer

A

There are multiple ring-enhancing lesions in both cerebral hemispheres with surrounding low attenuating areas consistent with white matter oedema.

B

The main differential of ring enhancing lesions in the brain is between tumour and infection (abscess). In view of the patient's history, tumour is the most likely cause because there is more than one lesion. Secondary deposits from her previous breast carcinoma is the most likely cause.

C

Oncological referral.
This would initially be for treatment of the white matter oedema with steroids.

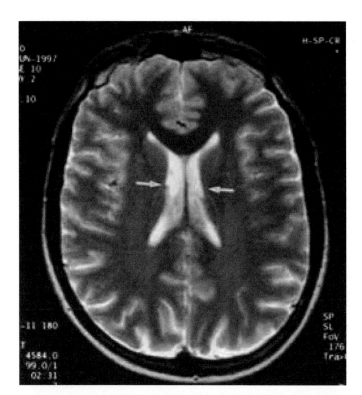

Figure 6a

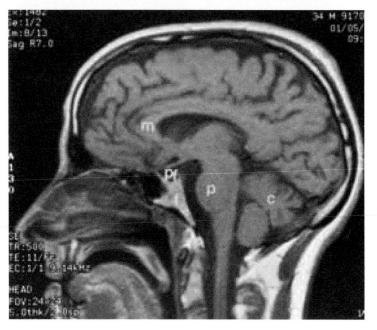

Figure 6b

A   *What are these studies?*
B   *How does it differ from a CT scan?*

Answer

A

a) Axial T2 weighted MR scan of the brain
   c   cerebellum   m corpus callosum
   p   pons   f   clivus
   pf pituitary fossa

b) This is a saggital T1-weighted MR scan of the brain.

B

MR is the abbreviation for magnetic resonance. As its name implies, the image is made by detecting resonance in a magnetic field. This resonance comes from freely moving protons. In bone, the protons are so tightly packed that they cannot move freely to generate a signal and so bone appears black. (An exception to this is some types of bone marrow which appear bright due to their fat content).

The T1 weighting can be determined by looking at the colour of the CSF. It appears dark on a T1-weighted image, and bright on a T2 image.

A CT scan is produced by passing X-rays through the patient and detecting the amount left. Depending on how much has been absorbed, the amount detected is assigned a grey scale and the computer builds up an image. Bone is dense and therefore absorbs a lot of X-rays preventing them from reaching the detectors. This area is shown as white. As mentioned above, bone is black on an MR scan.

Answer overleaf

A fit 30-year-old man presents with a sudden onset of lower back pain, bladder and bowel dysfunction and altered sensation, bowel and bladder disturbance. An urgent MR scan of the lumbar spine was performed.

Figure 7

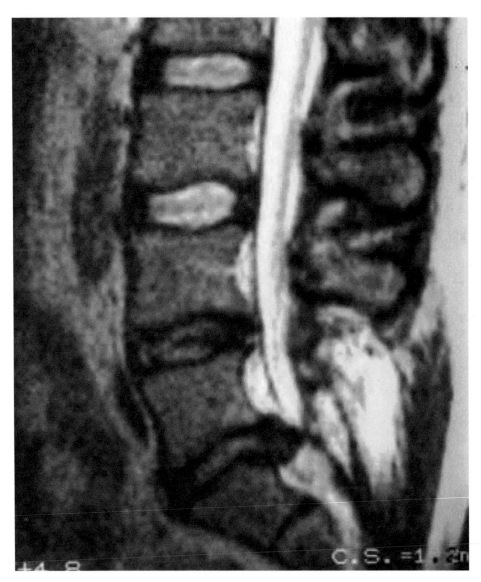

A   *What MR sequence and plane has been shown? Describe the abnormalities on the MR scan.*
B   *What is the diagnosis?*
C   *What is the next course of action?*

Answer

A
A T2 saggital image is shown of the lumbar sacral spine (T2 CSF is bright). There is decreased signal of the lower lumbar discs in keeping with degenerative dehydration. The L5/S1 disc is protruding posteriorly into the vertebral canal and compressing the nerve roots.

B
The diagnosis is **acute central disc prolapse with nerve compression.**

C
Urgent neurosurgical referral.

A 70-year-old man presents to his GP with a long history of decreasing intellect. A CT scan of the head was performed.

Figure 8

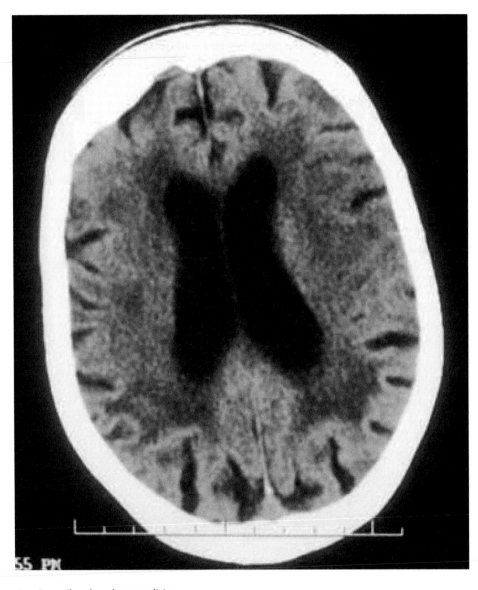

A   *Describe the abnormalities.*
B   *What is the diagnosis?*

Answer

A

There are two well defined low attenuating areas in the distribution of the left middle cerebral and right occipital vascular territory in keeping with old infarcts.

B

The diagnosis is **multi-infarct dementia.**

A 25-year-old female presents with primary infertility and galactorrhea.

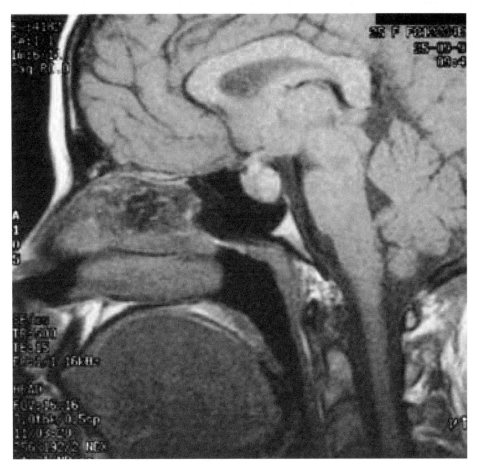

Figure 9

A *What imaging has been performed?*
B *Describe the abnormality.*
C *What is the diagnosis?*

Answer

A

A saggital brain T1-weighted MR scan without contrast has been performed (the image is T1 weighted as the CSF around the brain stem is of low signal; see case 13 page 131).

B

The pituitary fossa is enlarged with a high signal pituitary mass that extends up to the optic chiasm.

C

The diagnosis is a **pituitary macroadenoma** and in view of the clinical symptoms it is likely that it is a prolactinoma. Serum prolactin levels can be measured.

Answer
overleaf

A 30-year-old female with a past history of optic neuritis presents to neurology outpatients with difficulty in walking and incontinence.

Figure 10

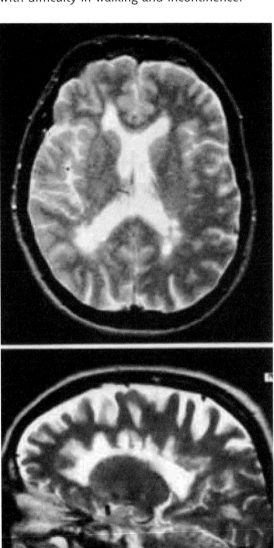

A   *What imaging has been performed?*
B   *Describe the abnormalities shown.*
C   *What is the most likely diagnosis?*
D   *What is the clinical definition that leads to this diagnosis?*

Answer

A
MR scan in axial and coronal plane of the brain with T2 weighting. (The CSF returns a high signal.)

B
Multiple small areas of high signal around the posterior horns of the lateral ventricles in the periventricular white matter on the axial image. Multiple areas of high signal in the corpus callosum extending to the ventricular margin.

C & D
In view of the patient's symptomatology (separate neurological events separated in time and space in the CNS), the patient's age and distribution of white matter lesions, **multiple sclerosis** is the most likely diagnosis.

A 50-year-old man presents with a gradual onset of unilateral hearing loss with headaches.

Figure 11

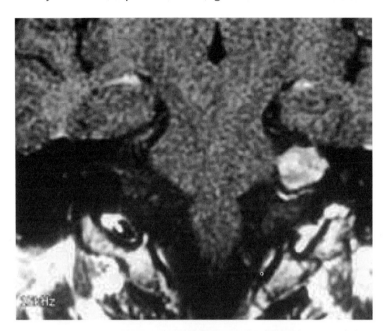

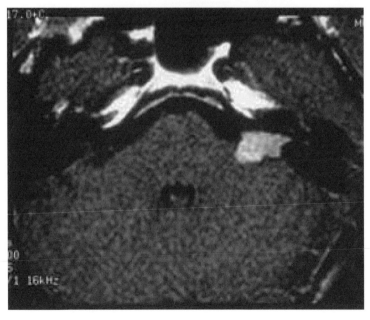

A   *What investigation has been performed?*
B   *Describe the abnormalities.*
C   *What is the diagnosis?*

Answer

A
A coronal and axial T1-weighted post contrast image of the posterior fossa.

B
A rounded 2 cm enhancing soft tissue mass in the left cerebellopontine angle. The mass originates from the VIII cranial nerve.

C
The diagnosis is a **left-sided acoustic neuroma**.

Answer overleaf

A 77-year-old woman is found on the floor by her daughter. She is confused and on examination she has a dysarthria and a right-sided weakness.

Figure 12

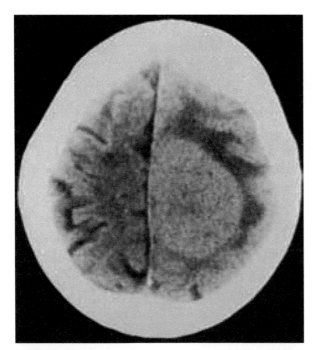

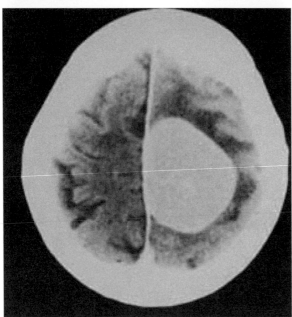

A   *Why has the scan been done twice?*
B   *What does the CT show?*

Answer

A

The CT scan has been performed twice, initially un-enhanced to look for haemorrhage and/or calcification, both of which show up as high density. Intravenous contrast medium appears as high density in blood vessels. It also appears as high density in the brain parenchyma itself if there is disruption of the blood brain barrier eg due to a tumour. It is therefore important to look at both scans as contrast medium may mask blood and calcification.

B

The CT scan shows a large well defined lesion in the left parietal lobe. It has an increased density compared to the surrounding brain, but is surrounded by low density oedema and there is mass effect with compression of the ipsilateral lateral ventricle. There is some calcification. The mass appears to arise from the falx. The post contrast scans demonstrate an homogeneous increase in density ie there is marked uniform enhancement.

These features are characteristic of a **meningioma**. Note that it arises from the dura ie is not a tumour of the brain parenchyma itself. The term extra-axial is sometimes used to describe this.

Answer overleaf

An 80-year old lady was found at home collapsed with profound right-sided weakness which occurred suddenly. Examination revealed a pyramidal (upper motor neurone weakness on the right) with brisk reflexes on the left and an up going plantar on the right. A CT brain was performed.

Figure 13

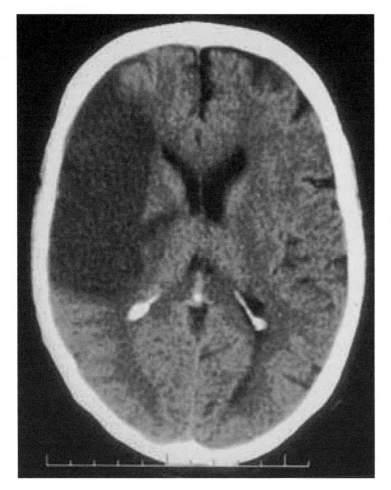

A   *Describe the abnormality.*
B   *What is the diagnosis?*
C   *What is the role of CT in this case?*

Answer

A

A well defined low attenuating lesion is seen in the left temporal lobe which involves the white and grey matter. Minimal mass effect is seen. There is no evidence of haemorrhage.

B

The diagnosis is a **right middle cerebral artery non-haemorrhagic infarct**.

C

CT confirms the diagnosis. If the infarct is non-haemorrhagic the patient can commence antiplatelet therapy such as aspirin, to try and improve perfusion to the affected area and to prevent occurence of other strokes.

Chapter 5
TRAUMA

A 30-year-old male is assaulted and brought to casualty by ambulance. On examination he has sustained head injuries with laceration of the scalp, he is conscious with no focal neurology. A skull series is performed.

Figure 1a

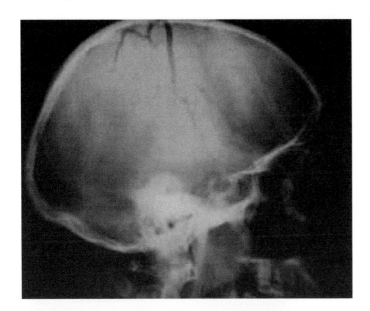

Figure 1b

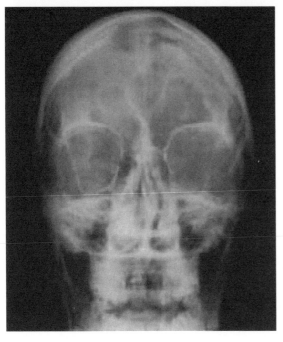

A *What abnormality is demonstrated on the skull X-rays?*
B *What is the further management of this patient?*

Answer

A

There are **multiple vault fractures** over the temporo-parietal region.

B

The patient should be admitted for neurological observations. If there is reduced level of consciousness or focal neurology development then an urgent CT scan of the brain should be performed to look for intracerebral haemorrhage.

The role of X-rays in skull trauma is to look for a vault fracture. Basal skull fractures are a clinical diagnosis. Fracture lines appear darker than vascular markings as they involve both the inner and outer skull vault tables. Fractures are straight lines which tend not to branch or taper unlike vessels.

A 23-year-old female is involved in a road traffic accident and brought to casualty complaining of severe neck pain. There is no focal neurology. The neck is immobilised and a cervical spine X-ray series performed.

Figure 2

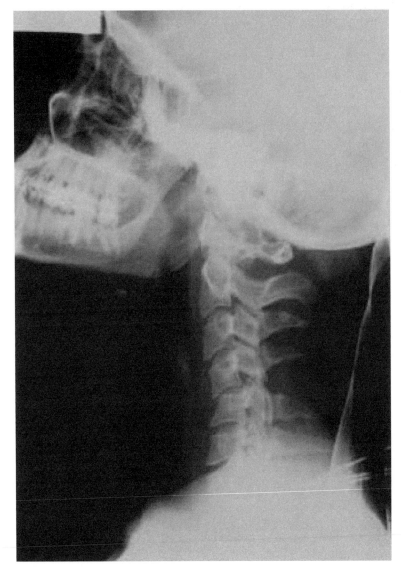

A   *Describe the abnormality on the lateral cervical spine film.*
B   *What is the further management of this patient?*

Answer

A

There is loss of the normal bony alignment with forward slip of C4 on C5 and widening of the interspinous distance between C4 and C5. The facet joints appear well aligned. This is typical of a **flexion injury** with disruption of the posterior longitudinal ligament and interspinous ligaments.

B

A CT through this area should be performed to look for fractures. The patient should be immobilised and a neurosurgical opinion advised.

A 23-year-old male riding a motorbike is involved in a road traffic incident and brought to casualty. Physical examination reveals a deformed right forearm. There was no other evidence of injury. An AP and lateral of the forearm was performed.

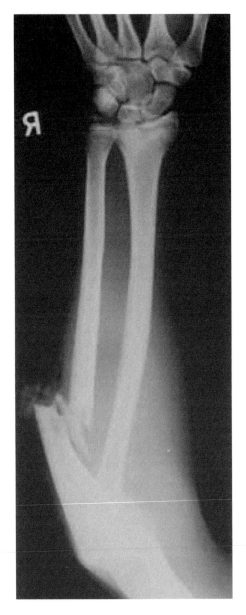

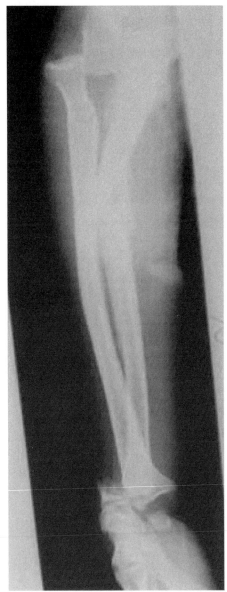

Figure 3a

Figure 3b

A   *Describe the abnormalities.*
B   *What is the name given to this fracture?*

Answer

A & B

There is a comminuted fracture of the ulna with dislocation of the radial head, which would be in keeping with a **Monteggia's fracture**. There is also a fracture of the distal end of the radius with dorsal displacement in keeping with **Colles' fracture**.

Answer
overleaf

A 17-year-old motorcyclist involved in a road traffic accident is brought to casualty with a painful right knee with limited range of movement. A series of knee X-rays are performed. A horizontal beam lateral is performed.

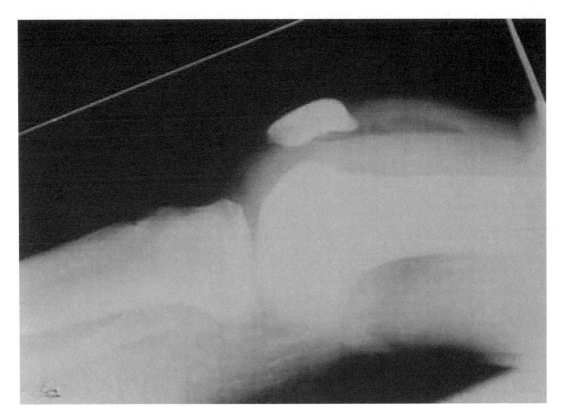

Figure 4

A   *Describe the abnormality.*
B   *What is the most likely cause?*

Answer

A

The patella is displaced anteriorly and there is a horizontal line with fat density above and soft tissue density below. This would be in keeping with a **lipohaemarthrosis**.

B

This is a fat fluid level from fat escaping from the marrow cavity and blood and would be indicative of bone injury. Close scrutinisation of the plain films is required. If no obvious bone injury is seen then a CT of the knee is required.

Answer
overleaf

An 80-year-old lady presents to casualty having fallen on to her outstretched hand. There is soft tissue swelling and deformity of the wrist with reduced range of movement at the wrist. An AP and lateral radiograph of the wrist is performed.

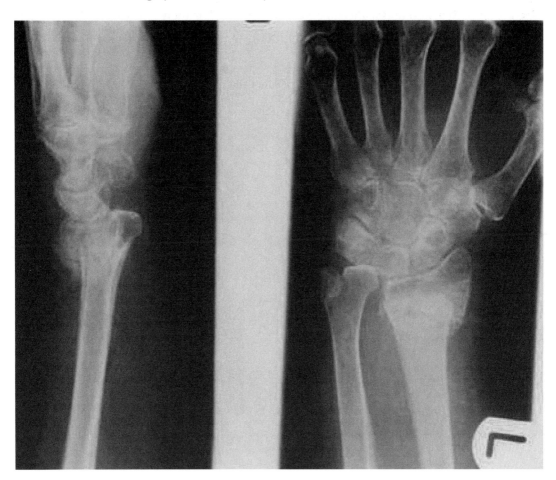

Figure 5

A   *Describe the X-ray abnormalities.*
B   *What is the diagnosis?*

Answer

A

There is impaction and dorsal angulation of the distal radius. There is also a fracture through the ulna styloid.

B

The appearance would be in keeping with a **Colles' fracture**. This fracture can be reduced using regional anaesthesia.

Answer overleaf

A 15-year-old boy presents to casualty having fallen on his outstretched hand. On examination there is decreased range of movement at the wrist. There is exquisite tenderness in the anatomical snuffbox. A radiograph of the wrist is performed with scaphoid views.

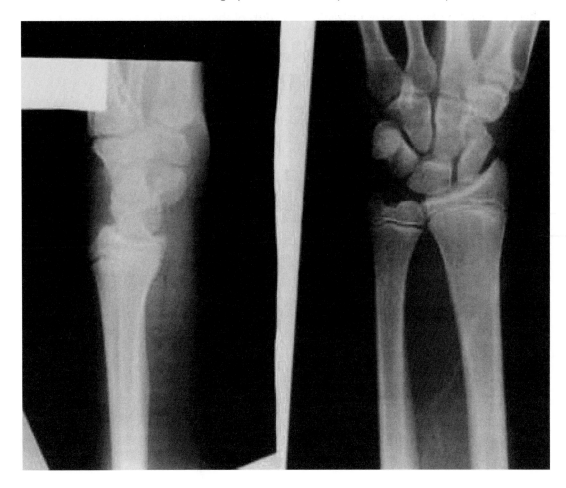

Figure 6

A *Describe the abnormality.*
B *What is the diagnosis?*

Answer

A
There is a lucency seen through the mid-pole (waist) of the scaphoid.

B
Scaphoid fracture
Immobilisation with a scaphoid plaster is required. If no fracture is seen but a scaphoid fracture is clinically suspected, a repeat X-ray series of the scaphoid should be performed after 10 to 14 days. This is because these fractures can sometimes be very difficult to see and there is a potentially disastrous consequence if a scaphoid fracture is missed. The proximal scaphoid receives its blood supply from the distal pole vessels and if the waist is fractured the **proximal** pole becomes avascular.

Answer overleaf

A 70-year-old lady presents to the Accident and Emergency department after falling onto her left hip; she has not been able to walk since. On examination the patient is in pain and has a shortened and externally rotated left leg.

Figure 7

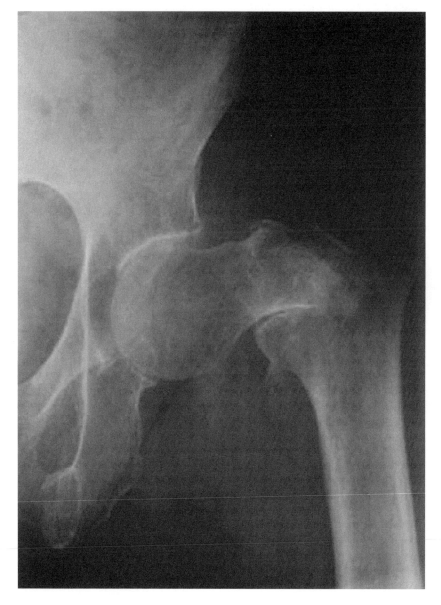

A   *Describe the X-ray abnormalities.*
B   *What is the diagnosis?*

Answer

A

There is a lucency through the neck of the left femur.

B

The diagnosis is a **fracture of the neck of the left femur**.

A 26-year-old male has been involved in a high speed road traffic accident. He is brought into the Accident and Emergency department unconscious and haemodynamically unstable.

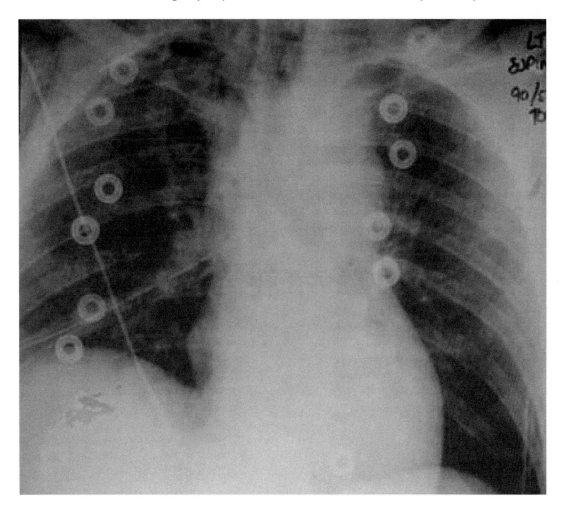

Figure 8

A *Describe the abnormality on the supine chest radiograph.*
B *What diagnosis should be confirmed or excluded?*

Answer

A

There is widening of the upper mediastinum due to haematoma seen on the supine chest radiograph.

B

Aortic transection should be suspected and helical contrasted enhanced CT of the thorax should be performed.

Answer
overleaf

An eight-year-old girl fell in the playground at school on to her outstretched hand. She has pain and tenderness over the distal radius. A plain X-ray of the wrist is taken.

Figure 9

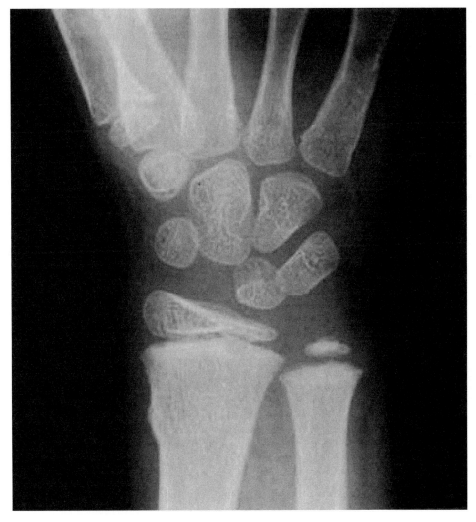

A *Describe the X-ray abnormalities.*
B *What is the diagnosis?*

Answer

A
On the lateral aspect of the distal radius there is an abnormal cortical outline with buckling of the cortex. No definite fracture line can be seen.

B
The diagnosis is a **greenstick fracture of the distal radius**. The bones of the developing skeleton are elastic and may bend rather than break. This gives rise to abnormal critical outlines after trauma.

A 20-year-old patient presented at casualty after a fall on the outstretched hand with pain in the elbow and limited range of movement of flexion extension, pronation and supination. A plain radiograph, with two views is taken.

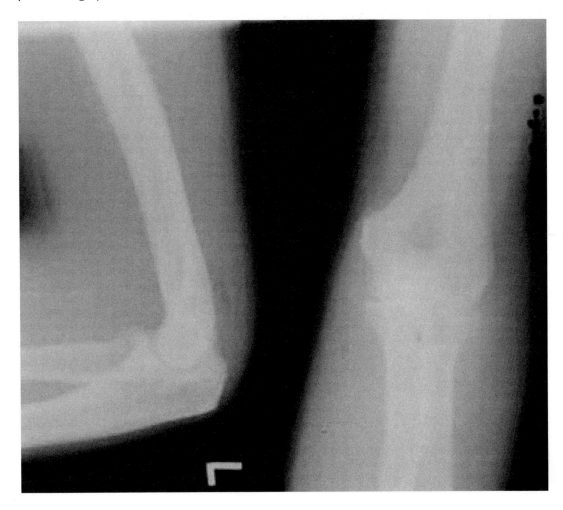

Figure 10

A   *Describe the abnormalities.*

B   *What is the diagnosis?*

Answer

A

On the lateral film there are lucencies in the soft tissue. On the anterior aspect and posterior aspect of the distal humerus on the lateral represent fat pads which overlie the joint capsule. These are lifted away from the distal humerus in the presence of a joint effusion, a so called 'fat pads signs'. There is a step irregularity of the cortex of the radial head.

B

The diagnosis is a **radial neck fracture with elbow joint effusion**.

Chapter 6
PAEDIATRICS

A baby was born at term by Caesarean section for a breech presentation. When the toddler was 3-years-old his parents became concerned that he was still not walking properly.

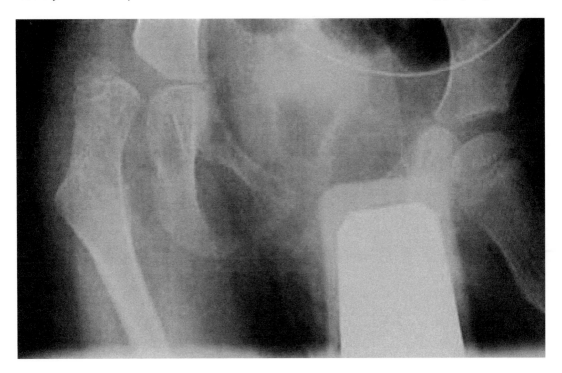

Figure 1

A   *What does the pelvic X-ray show?*
B   *Could this have been avoided?*

Answer
overleaf

A 4-year-old child presents with a painful hip. On examination his left hip is painful and he cannot fully weight-bear on it. He is afebrile and otherwise well.

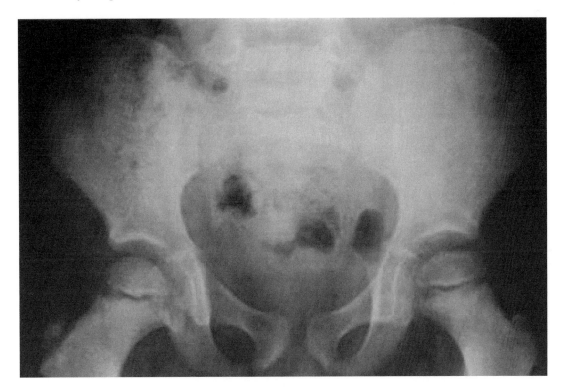

Figure 2a

A   *What are the possible causes of the pain?*
B   *What does the pelvic X-ray above show?*

Answer

A

The possible causes for a painful hip include **infection** and **Perthes' disease**. **Septic arthritis** is an important diagnosis to consider, especially if the child is pyrexial and systemically unwell. Untreated it will cause rapid joint destruction, affecting BOTH the femoral head and acetabulum, ie it crosses and affects both sides of the joint space.

Perthes' disease commonly occurs in children between 4 and 10 years of age. It is more common in boys than girls, with a ratio of 5:1. Perthes' disease is avascular necrosis of the femoral head.

There are many other causes of avascular necrosis but when it occurs in this age group and there is no other cause, the term Perthes' is used.

B

On the pelvic X-ray, small lucencies can be seen in the superior aspect of the left femoral head which are due to ischaemia resulting in bone death. Note that the acetabulum is NOT affected as this is a process that is confined to the femoral head. If left untreated, the femoral head may be destroyed (see below).

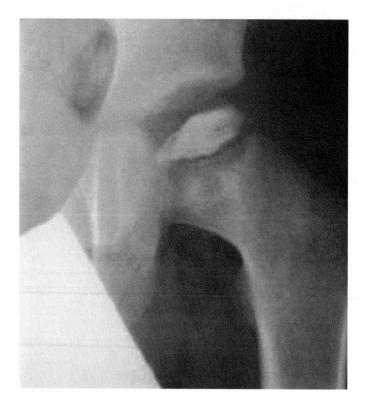

Figure 2b

A 12-year-old girl presents with a painful left hip.

Figure 3

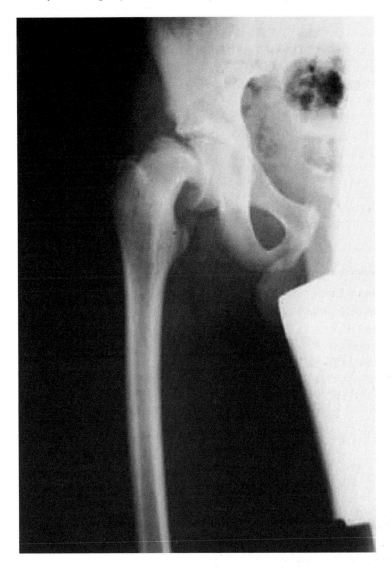

A   *What are the possible diagnoses?*
B   *What does the pelvic X-ray show?*
C   *What other X-ray should be obtained?*

Answer

A

The most important diagnoses to consider are **slipped femoral capital epiphyses** if the patient is afebrile and septic arthritis if the patient is febrile and systemically unwell.

B

On the pelvic radiograph note the following features of slipped capital (proximal) femoral epiphyses:

▪ The height of the femoral head is reduced.
▪ The epiphysis is irregular and reduced in height.
▪ A line drawn along the lateral margin of the femoral neck does not pass through the epiphysis of the femoral head compared with the normal side.

C

A lateral view should be obtained. Many slips do not show on the AP film and will be missed if a lateral is not performed, leading to permanent damage to the hip.

The condition affects an older age group than Perthes'. The patients are usually between 10 and 15 years of age. It is slightly more common in girls. Treatment usually involves pinning the epiphysis and removing the pins when fusion has taken place. Both hips should be followed up in every case as the condition is bilateral in up to 25% of patients.

A 20-month-old child is brought into casualty by ambulance; he is breathless and cyanosed. His parents say he had been playing with his older brother and had been very well that day and the breathlessness came on suddenly. On examination the boy is cyanosed and tachypnoeic. The right side of his chest is not moving and there is tracheal deviation to the right.

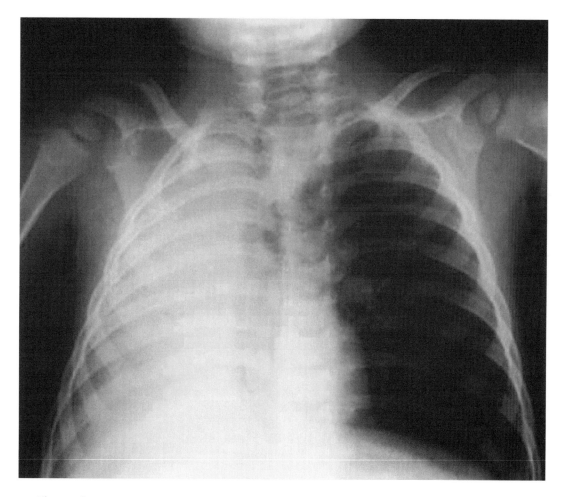

Figure 4

A   *What does the chest X-ray show?*
B   *What is the diagnosis?*
C   *What is your management?*

Answer

A

The chest X-ray shows complete opacification of the right hemithorax.
There is volume loss of the right hemithorax. Signs of volume loss include:

- Mediastinal shift (the trachea and heart are deviated to the right).
- Rib crowding (the ribs are closer together than on the other side).
- Elevation of the hemidiaphragm (in this case this is difficult to appreciate because the whole lung is affected).
- The left lung has expanded to compensate and this can be appreciated as a lucency behind the heart.

B

The diagnosis is **collapse of the right lung,** which in this age group is likely to be due to an inhaled foreign body, eg peanut or other food or a small toy.

C

The management consists of immediate referral to a respiratory physician for urgent bronchoscopy and removal of the foreign body.

A baby is born prematurely at 32 weeks. Two hours after delivery the baby becomes breathless and this increases in severity. The baby is intubated and ventilated.

Figure 5

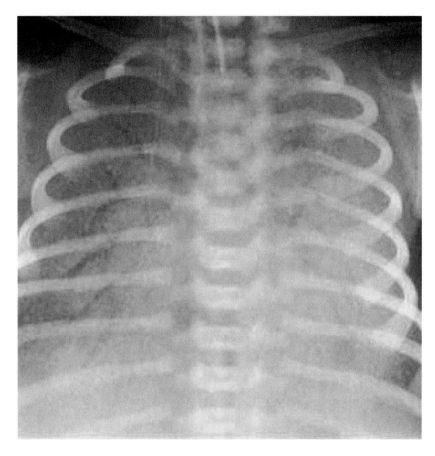

A   *What does the chest X-ray show?*

Answer

There is an endotracheal tube, which lies at an appropriate position at the level of the clavicles.

There is widespread air space shadowing and air bronchograms.

These are the features of **hyaline membrane disease** due to surfactant deficiency in respiratory distress of the newborn. Atelactasis, which produces volume loss, is another feature but this is not present in this case as the baby is ventilated.

An 11-year-old boy presents with recurrent chest infections. He has a chronic cough productive of thick sputum.

Figure 6

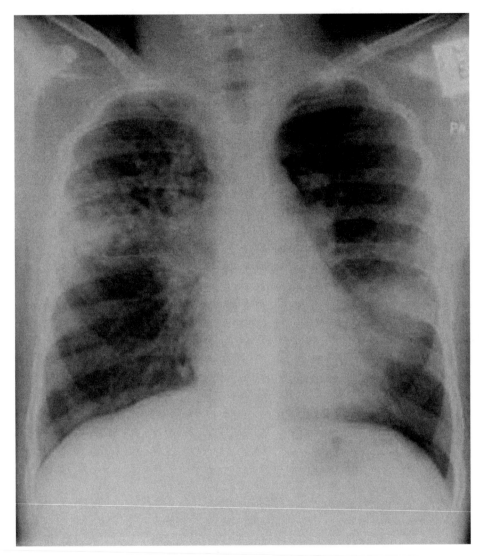

A   *What does the chest X-ray show?*
B   *What is the likely diagnosis?*
C   *What are the other features of this condition?*

Answer

A

There are abnormalities of the right upper lobe with peribronchial cuffing, suggestive of bronchiectasis. There is also consolidation of the left mid-zone.

B

The likely diagnosis is **cystic fibrosis.**

C

Cystic fibrosis is a multi-system disease. Mucous plugging of exocrine glands occurs due to abnormal mucociliary function and production of abnormally viscous secretions by exocrine gland dysfunction. The cystic fibrosis gene is on chromosome 7 and is inherited in an autosomal recessive manner.

Systems that are affected include:

GI tract
▪ Meconium ileus, rectal prolapse, chronic constipation, gastro-oesophageal reflux and failure to thrive.

Liver and biliary tree
▪ Biliary cirrhosis, portal hypertension, gallstones.

Pancreas
▪ Steatorrhoea, malabsorption, abdominal pain, bloating, failure to thrive.
▪ Diabetes mellitus, acute and chronic pancreatitis.

Skull
▪ Sinusitis.

GU
▪ Failure of transport of sperm leading to infertility.

Answer overleaf

A 6-day-old baby is taken to the casualty department with recurrent abdominal pain and vomiting. On examination she is dehydrated and distressed. She is referred to the surgeons who consider the diagnosis of a malrotation. A barium meal study is requested.

Figure 7

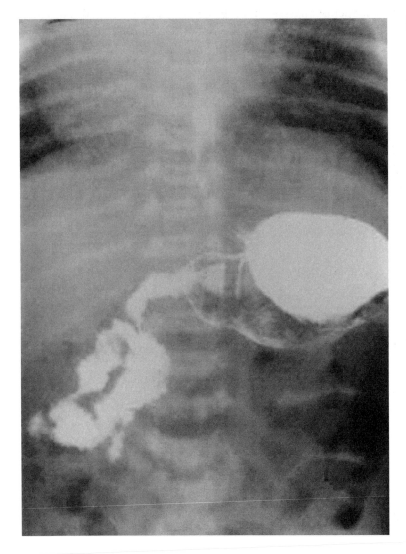

A   *What does the barium meal show?*
B   *What is the management?*

Answer

A

Normally the third part of the duodenum passes horizontally across the midline so that the third part of the duodenum can be seen to the left of the vertebral column. In this case the bowel is to the right because of failure of the normal rotation that occurs in utero.

B

The baby requires immediate resuscitation and surgery.

A one-year-old child presents with a urinary tract infection.

A   *What is your radiological management?*

Answer

A

All children under five years of age with a proven urinary tract infection need investigating. Investigations are aimed at identifying an underlying cause and assessing/monitoring the damage that has occurred. Investigations may also help determine the type of treatment needed, eg surgery may be useful (in cases of reflux, reimplantation of the ureters may prevent further damage).

Ultrasound

This is an important, non-invasive method of examining structural abnormalities such as hydronephrosis, horseshoe kidney, ectopic kidney and duplex systems, all of which may predispose to infection. Renal stones may also be detected. Ultrasound may also demonstrate scars in the kidney which are the consequence of reflux/infection, but DMSA scans are better at demonstrating scars.

Nuclear medicine scans (These tests assess function.)

DMSA tests demonstrate scars. The isotope becomes fixed in the proximal convoluted tubules of the kidney and does not enter the ureters and bladder. This is in contrast to the other isotopes used such as DTPA and MAG3. DTPA is freely filtered and enters the tubules, collecting system and then the ureters and bladder. If reflux of urine occurs, this will be seen as activity in the ureters or kidney after bladder activity was seen. Normally, once activity is seen in the bladder it should not be seen elsewhere in the urinary tract. MAG3 provides similar information to DTPA but can be better in that it is actively secreted into the proximal convoluted tubules, providing a higher percentage of isotope in the kidney.

Micturating cystourethrogram

This may be done under X-ray guidance, or with a nuclear medicine isotope.

X-ray guided studies involve catheter insertion into the bladder which is then filled with an iodine based contrast medium which shows up with X-rays. A full bladder stimulates the child to micturate and when this commences, the catheter is removed. Contrast should not be seen in the ureters or kidneys; its presence indicates reflux.

A nuclear medicine isotope can be instilled into the bladder via a catheter and reflux detected using a gamma camera. If a child is old enough to micturate when asked, an indirect cystourethrogram can be performed. An injection of isotope is given which is cleared by the kidneys and enters the ureters and bladder. This avoids the use of a catheter and is more physiological.

Answer overleaf

A seven-year-old boy presented to casualty via his GP with a six-week history of severe headache which was worse in the mornings and exacerbated by coughing or sneezing. His mother has also noted that he was unsteady on his feet. On examination the patient had bilateral papilloedema and cerebellar signs.

Figure 9

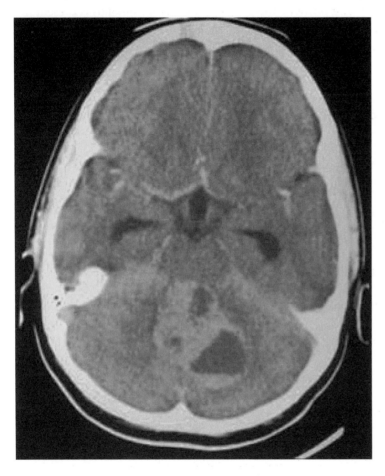

A *Describe the abnormality.*
B *What is the differential diagnosis?*

Answer

A

There is a large 4 cm mass which is well circumscribed with areas of high and low attenuation centred on the fourth ventricle in the posterial fossa. Obstructive hydrocephalus is present as the temporal horns of the lateral ventricles are dilated. There were no other lesions seen on the brain scan.

B

The differential diagnosis for this solitary lesion centred on the fourth ventricle is a primary glioma such as **medulloblastoma, ependymona or astrocytoma.**

Answer overleaf

A one-year-old boy presented to casualty as an emergency with a history of intermittent screaming associated and bleeding per rectum. This stool has the appearance of redcurrant jelly. Plain film was unhelpful and an ultrasound was requested.

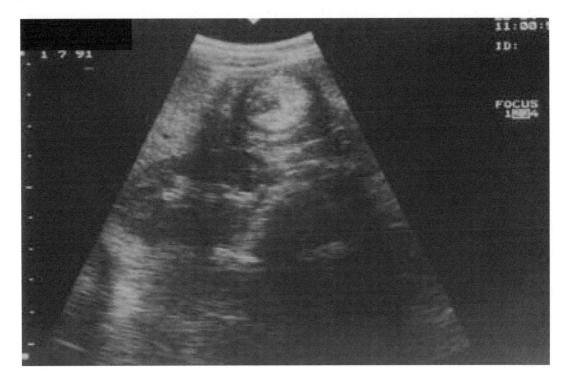

Figure 10

A   *What does the ultrasound show?*
B   *What is the treatment of choice?*

Answer

A

The ultrasound scan shows a '**target**' and '**doughnut**' sign which is the classical appearance of an intussusception. An intussusception is the invagination of one segment of bowel into another. It is usually ileo-colic (the ileum invaginates into colon). The condition has a high mortality and must be treated immediately.

B

If the patient is clinically well the treatment is reduction of the intussusception with either barium or air *per rectum* (air is more commonly used as it is safer if bowel perforation occurs). If this fails or the child is clinically unwell, surgery is required.

Answer overleaf

A female infant is brought to casualty with symptoms and signs of a chest infection. The child was unkempt. X-rays are performed.

Figure 11a

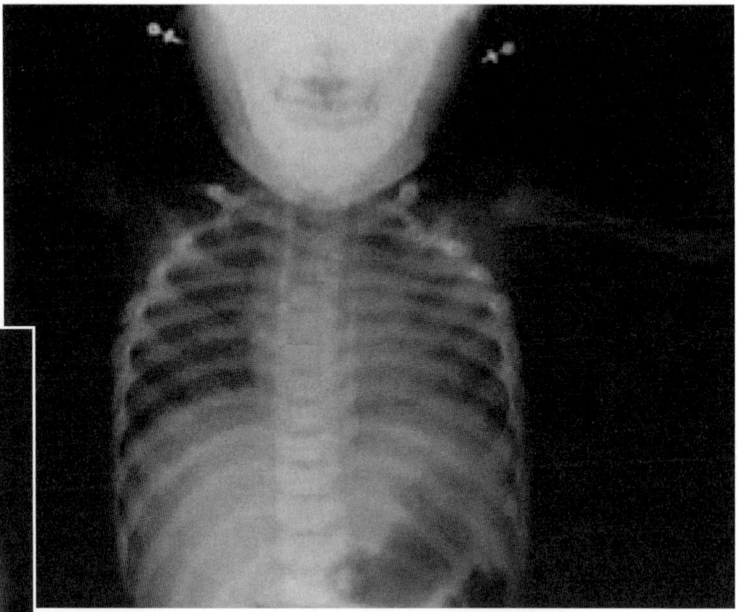

Figure 11b

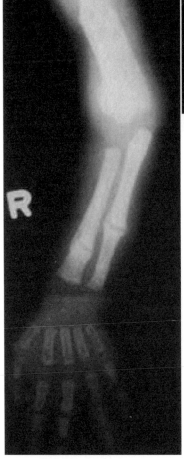

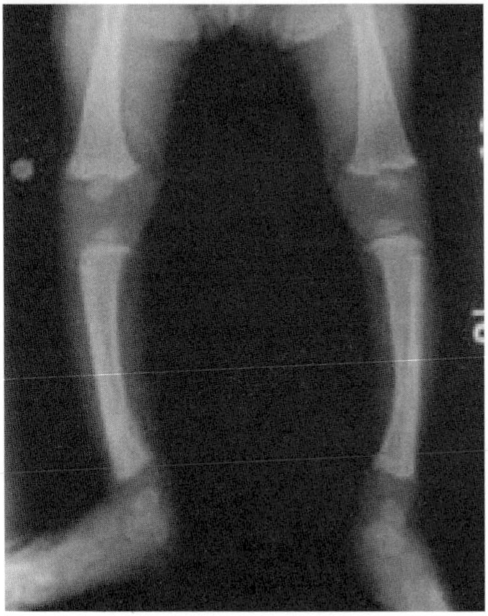

Figure 11c

A *Describe the abnormalities.*
B *What is the diagnosis?*

Answer

A

There is marked periosteal reaction of the left humerus and re-modelling abnormality of the right humerus in keeping with previous fractures. There is a healing fracture of the right radius and ulna. Multiple posterior rib fractures are seen at various stages of healing.

B

The presence of healing fractures at various stages and posterior rib fractures is a classical indication of **non-accidental injury**.

Test Paper 1

INTRODUCTION

Before doing the test papers remember a few important principles. Firstly knowing the diagnosis is the LEAST important part of answering the question and, in fact, carries the least marks. What is more important is the description. It is important to write down what the investigation is, even if the question does not specifically ask for this.

When describing an X-ray try and comment on the projection, eg AP or PA (or if you are unsure just use the term frontal). If there are artefacts, eg ECG or monitor lines, mention them and if there are internal lines also comment on them and specifically look to make sure they are in the correct position with no complication, eg pneumothorax.

The abnormalities should be described next. Do not forget to state which side the abnormality is as you will not only lose valuable marks if you do not, but in real life the consequence may be life-threatening. Finally try to draw a conclusion; this may be a diagnosis or a differential diagnosis and in the case of the latter, list them in the order in which they most commonly occur (put the rarest condition at the bottom).

NB: Numbers shown at the end of questions in this section indicate marks given in the examination.

15 Questions: Time allowed 45 minutes

A 73-year-old male has a three month history of increasing inappropriate behaviour and loss of inhibition.

(a) *What is this examination?*
(b) *What is the technical difference between the two images?*
(c) *Describe the findings.*
(d) *What is the likely diagnosis?*

These are two images from a CT of the brain.

Figure 1a

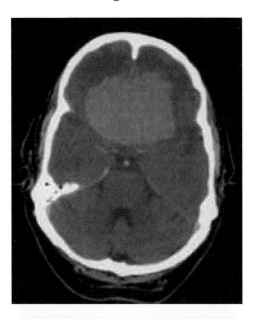

Figure 1b

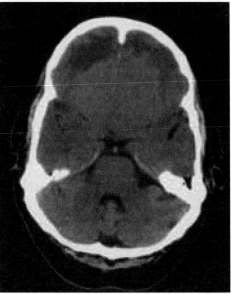

Answer

The scans have been obtained before and after intravenous contrast enhancement. Intravenous contrast crosses an abnormal blood-brain barrier and a lesion may enhance diffusely as here or may enhance in a ring-like manner.

There is a large enhancing mass lesion lying in the anterior cranial fossa and surrounding this lesion there is a rim of compressed brain of lower density than normal consistent with oedema in the frontal lobes, which is the result of a significant mass effect.

The most likely diagnosis of this large space-occupying lesion is a slow growing meningioma. Meningiomas typically have a diffuse intense enhancement following intravenous contrast and there is often quite marked oedema of the adjacent brain substance. This is likely to be arising from the falx cerebri lying in the midline. The patient's inappropriate behaviour is due to bilateral frontal lobe damage.

This is a 52-year-old lady with a long history of pain, swelling and deformity of her joints.

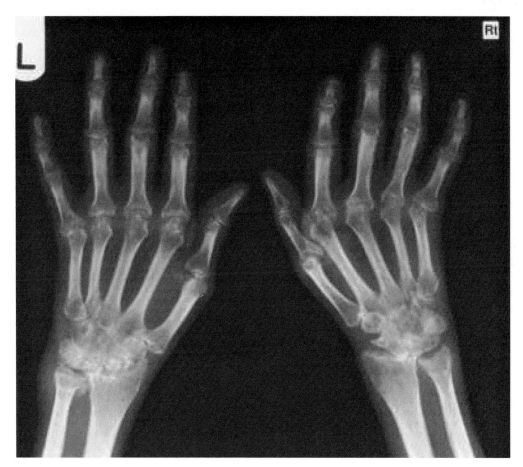

Figure 2

(a) *Describe the abnormalities seen on this film.*
(b) *What is the differential diagnosis?*
(c) *What other investigation would help in making the diagnosis?*

Answer

There is quite marked periarticular osteoporosis and there are multiple erosions of the wrist joints, metacarpo-phalangeal joints and the proximal interphalangeal joints. There is ulnar deviation of the fingers and subluxation of several of the metacarpo-phalangeal joints. The wrist joints show extensive loss of joint margins and destruction of some of the carpal bones and there is also erosive change at the distal radio-ulnar joint on the left. In addition soft tissue swelling is seen around the distal ulna on the left.

The differential diagnosis is between erosive arthropathies which will include rheumatoid arthritis, psoriatic arthropathy and gout. The distribution of the erosive changes in this patient and the ulnar deviation and the destruction of the carpal joints is typical of rheumatoid arthritis. In psoriatic arthropathy the changes are not so symmetrical as here and there is a tendency for the distal interphalangeal joints to be affected. Also in psoriatic arthropathy the bone mineralisation is maintained. In gout the erosive changes are periarticular rather than involving the joint line.

Immunological investigation will show a positive rheumatoid factor (an IgM immunoglobulin) in over 80% of cases of rheumatoid arthritis.

An 85-year-old lady presents with abdominal pain and a palpable abdominal mass.

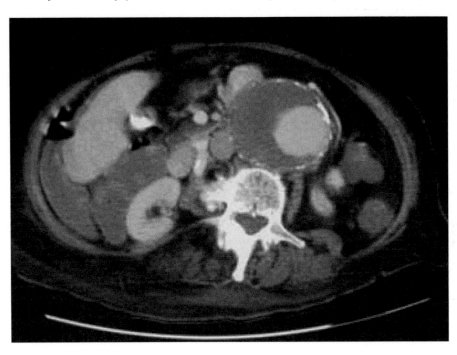

Figure 3

(a) *What is this investigation?*
(b) *What does it show?*
(c) *What is the usual aetiology of this?*
(d) *State two complications that may be seen on imaging.*

Answer

This is a contrast-enhanced CT scan of the abdomen. The right kidney is enhanced and the lumen of the aorta is also enhanced.

There is an abdominal aortic aneurysm which has a maximum diameter of 8 cm. The wall of the aneurysm is calcified and between the wall and the enhancing lumen there is lower density material which is thrombus.

Abdominal aortic aneuysms are usually the result of artherosclerosis.

The major complications of abdominal aortic aneurysms are rupture, infection and fistulation into the adjacent bowel. Abdominal aortic rupture may be seen on imaging when contrast is seen outside the lumen of the aorta. Infection may be demonstrated if there is air within the aneurysmal sac. Fistulation may be seen if there is contrast entering adjacent loops of bowel.

Abdominal aortic aneurysms which are greater then 5.5 cm diameter have a rupture rate of about 10% per annum and therefore require surgical or endovascular repair.

Answer
overleaf

An 85-year-old man with long-standing back pain presented with a new episode of back pain.

Figure 4a

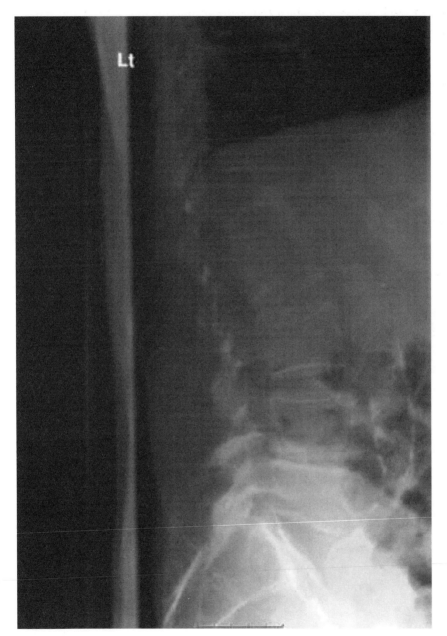

(a) *What three abnormalities are seen on this film?*
(b) *What further radiological investigation would you request?*
(c) *What is the differential diagnosis for the acute episode?*

Answer

This is a lateral lumbar spine radiograph which shows three abnormalities which can present with back pain. There is narrowing of the disc space at the L4–5 level with some associated osteophyte formation at the margins of the L4–5 disc space. This is consistent with degenerative disc disease. There is also calcification in the abdominal aorta which would make one suspicious of the presence of an abdominal aortic aneurysm which may also give rise to back pain.

The body of the first lumbar vertebra had collapsed and has assumed a wedge shape. The bone density of the vertebral body is also reduced. This was the cause of the acute episode of back pain and the differential diagnosis would include a metastasis, vertebral collapse due to a myeloma deposit or a traumatic vertebral compression fracture although the loss of bone density is against this. A vertebral body fracture due to osteoporosis is unusual in a man.

Further evaluation of the lesion in the L1 vertebral body should be either a radioisotope bone scan to look for other lesions which would suggest metastatic disease or further investigation with an MR scan. This patient underwent MR imaging of the spine (Fig 4b).

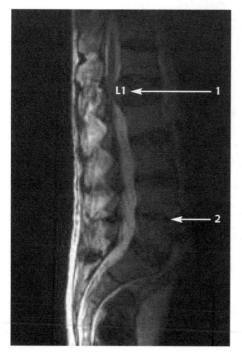

Figure 4b

This showed that the body of L1 had completely collapsed and had extruded posteriorly where it was impressing on the spinal cord (arrow 1). A CT-guided biopsy of the vertebral body revealed metastatic squamous cell carcinoma from a primary lung tumour. The narrowed L4-5 disc space is also seen on the MR scan (arrow 2).

Answer
overleaf

A 37-year-old marathon runner presented with pain in the foot for one month.

Figure 5

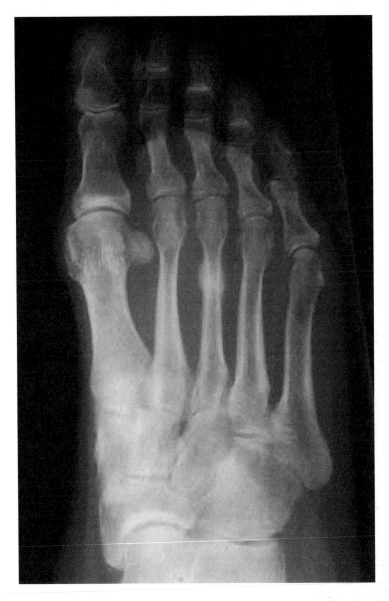

(a) *Describe the radiological appearance and abnormality.*
(b) *What is the mechanism of the disease process?*
(c) *How should he be managed clinically?*

Answer

The neck of the third metacarpal is expanded and thickened by periosteal new bone formation and the cortex has become expanded.

This is a stress fracture and the periosteal new bone formation is the healing process. Stress fractures occur from chronic stress forces which would not fracture a bone by themselves but when repeated over time result in a stress fracture. The new bone formation around the site of the fracture may be the only abnormality detected radiologically. MR imaging may be of value in establishing the diagnosis before plain film signs of a stress fracture are apparent.

The patient should be advised to rest until the fracture has completely healed.

A 62-year-old gentleman, with a known history of chronic alcohol abuse, presents to this GP with a four month history of bouts of epigastric pain radiating to the back which is relieved by leaning forwards. He has also noticed that his stools have become more offensive. Urine dipstick reveals the presence of glucose.

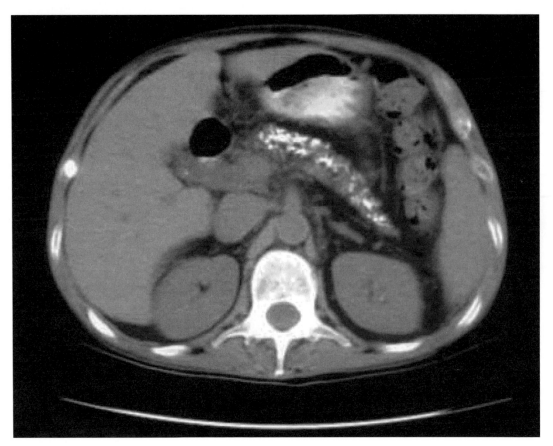

Figure 6

(a) *What is this investigation?*
(b) *What are the higher density areas in the liver parenchyma?*
(c) *What is the significant abnormality on this examination?*
(d) *What is the most likely diagnosis and the most likely cause?*

Answer

This is an abdominal CT scan with intravenous contrast enhancement. The aorta, inferior vena cava and other vascular structures and the kidney are of increased density due to intravenous contrast administration. The CT scan has been obtained about 70 seconds after the intravenous injection of contrast. There is also some contrast seen in the stomach. Oral contrast agents are used to opacify the stomach and small bowel loops.

The higher density areas in the liver parenchyma are contrast-enhanced branches of the hepatic portal vein and the hepatic veins.

The abnormality is discrete foci of calcification throughout the body and tail of the pancreas and the pancreas itself is moderately atrophic. There is no pancreatic duct dilatation.

This appearance is due to chronic calcific pancreatitis and this is the most common form of chronic pancreatitis seen in the developed world. It is usually caused by alcohol and in general alcohol consumption will have been above 150 g (about 20 units) per day for more than 10 years. A high protein diet, sometimes with a high fat content, may potentiate the effect of alcohol.

Offensive stools result from an increase in the fat content giving rise to steatorrhoea. This occurs when the secretion of pancreatic lipase is reduced in pancreatic disease. The steatorrhoea is often severe and the patient may notice drops of fat in the lavatory pan. It occurs in about half of patients with chronic pancreatitis.

Glucosuria, as demonstrated on urine dipstick, results from the development of diabetes. Transient Type II diabetes is a common finding associated with chronic pancreatitis.

Answer
overleaf

A 78-year-old gentleman presented to his GP with lower back pain. For several months he had difficulty passing urine and had recently lost some weight. On examination, there was local tenderness over the sacrum with numbness over the posterior aspect of the right thigh and heel. Rectal examination revealed a palpable hard, irregular mass. This examination was part of the diagnostic work up.

Figure 7

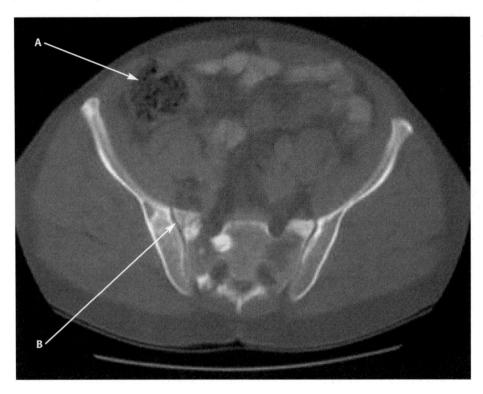

(a) *What is this examination and how is the image presented?*
(b) *What is arrow (a) pointing at?*
(c) *What is arrow (b) pointing at?*
(d) *What is the abnormality seen?*
(e) *What is the most likely diagnosis?*

Answer

This is a CT scan through the pelvis, which has been grey scaled (window setting) to demonstrate bony detail.

Arrow (a) is pointing at the caecum containing faecal matter.

Arrow (b) is pointing at the right sacroiliac joint.

The abnormality is several areas of higher density in the sacrum and lateral to the right sacroiliac joint. These have the appearance of sclerotic metastases.

The most likely diagnosis is adenocarcinoma of the prostate with sclerotic bony metastases. Commonly in metastatic bone disease such as is seen in breast cancer, the lesions in bone are lytic where bone substance is actually destroyed. Bony metastases from prostate cancer however are usually sclerotic; lytic metastases from prostate cancer are extremely rare.

CT is used in the staging of prostate cancer, looking for spread of disease to pelvic lymph nodes in particular. When viewing these scans it is important to look at the images on both soft tissue and bone window settings.

A 65-year-old male who had had a right hemi-colectomy for colonic cancer was receiving chemotherapy on the oncology day-unit for two metastatic lesions in his liver. In order to assess the effectiveness of the chemotherapy he had this CT scan performed.

Figure 8

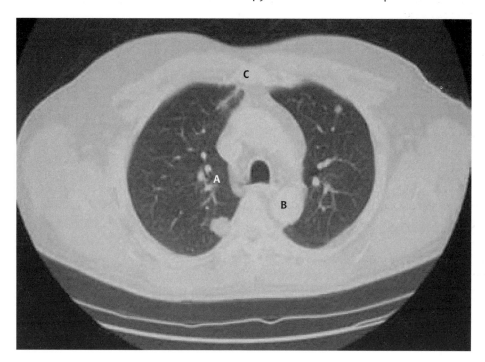

(a) *Which area of the body is this section from?*
(b) *What has the grey scale been set to demonstrate?*
(c) *What is the structure labelled 'a'?*
(d) *What is the structure labelled 'b'?*
(e) *What is the structure labelled 'c'?*
(f) *What abnormality is seen?*

Answer

This is a CT section taken through the lower thorax.

The grey scale (window setting) has been selected to show the lung parenchyma. The thorax is usually imaged with two different grey scale settings: One for the mediastinal structures and one for the lung parenchyma.

'a' is a right lower lobe bronchus.

'b' is the descending aorta.

'c' is the sternum

The abnormality seen is two rounded mass lesions in both lower zones. These are well demarcated lesions and with such well defined margins are most likely to be metastases.

In colon-rectal cancer lung metastases are usually seen in the liver first. Lung metastases are rarely seen without the presence of liver metastases.

A 44-year-old cyclist was involved in an accident and went over the handlebars and landed on his hands. He had pain in the elbow and all movement of the forearm was limited.

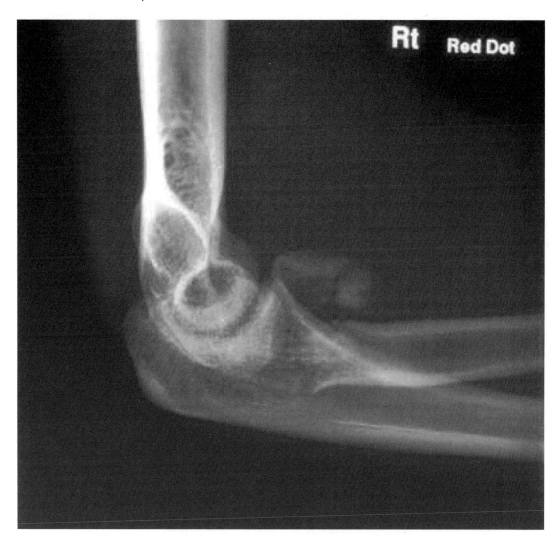

Figure 9a

(a) *Describe the abnormality shown on this radiograph.*
(b) *How might this be managed?*

Answer

The radius has been fractured and the radial head has become separated from the radial shaft. It has dislocated so much that it is now lying at a right angle to its normal articulation with the capitulum.

Fracture of the radial head and neck generally results from a fall on the outstretched hand. The impact of the fall drives the radial head axially onto the capitulum of the humerus. Pain and an effusion in the elbow as well as tenderness on palpation directly over the radial head are typical signs. Often the injury only results in a crack through the radial head which can be managed conservatively.

Figure 9b

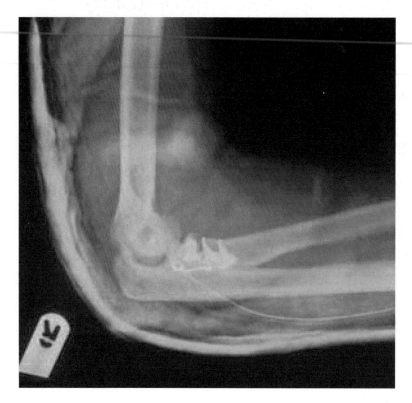

In this situation with the dislocation of the separated head of the radius, there would also have been ligamentous damage and surgical repair was undertaken (Fig 9b).

A 63-year-old lady, extremely short of breath, had to be admitted to the intensive care unit for management of severe respiratory dysfunction. This is the chest radiograph taken on the unit.

Figure 10

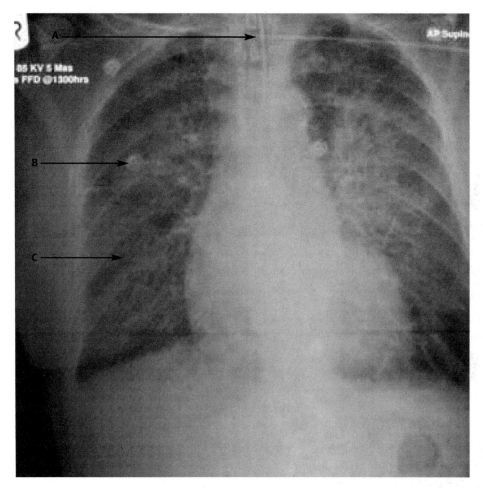

(a) *What is arrow 'a' pointing at?*
(b) *What is arrow 'b' pointing at?*
(c) *What is arrow 'c' pointing at?*
(d) *What process is going on in the lungs?*

Answer

'a' is an endotracheal tube. The patient is being ventilated. The tip of the endotracheal tube should be 2–3 cm above the tracheal bifurcation. If an endotracheal tube is inserted too far down the trachea it can end up in the right or left main bronchus and result in non-ventilation of an entire lung.

'b' is an electrocardiograph electrode. Several of these are applied to the anterior chest to monitor cardiac activity.

'c' is a lymphatic or septal line. These are sometimes referred to as Kerley lines.

In the lungs there is extensive diffuse opacity spreading out from both hila into the lungs. The appearances are more prominent in the left lung than the right. In addition there are multiple fine linear opacities seen peripherally which represent septal lines (arrow 'c'). These appearances are those of pulmonary oedema. In heart failure as the pulmonary venous pressure increases the lung also increases in stiffness as a result of fluid leakage out into the interstitium of the lungs. This fluid has to drain back into the circulation via intrapulmonary lymphatics which become more prominent and are seen as the septal lines.

Answer
overleaf

An 84-year-old lady has been under regular review for many years in the Chest Clinic. This is a recent follow-up chest radiograph.

Figure 11a

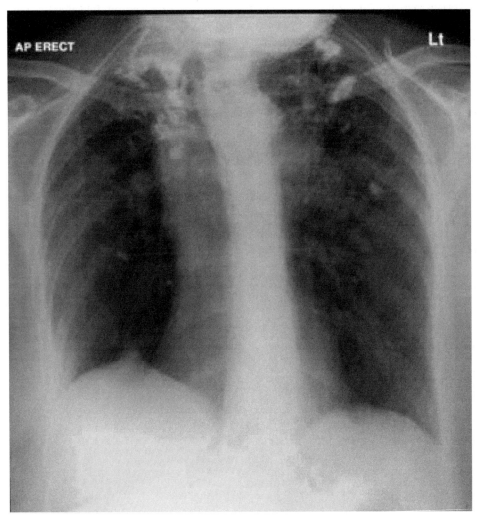

(a) *Describe the appearances.*
(b) *What disease process has produced these appearances?*

Answer

There is extensive volume loss of both upper lobes which has resulted in the hila being dragged upwards to the upper part of both hemithoraces. The left pulmonary artery (A) is much higher than normal. The right lower lobe pulmonary artery (B) is also much higher than normal. The outline of the superior mediastinum is also lost and the aortic arch is not clearly seen. This is the end result of extensive fibrosis of both upper lobes. There is also thickening of the pleura at the right apex (C). In addition there are multiple calcified opacities in both upper lobes (D). There is also deviation of the trachea over to the right.

These appearances are the result of tuberculosis. When tuberculous consolidation and cavitation heals it results in fibrosis and volume loss. Cavities have been obliterated with the fibrosis. Since the upper lobes are most commonly involved by tuberculosis the contraction results in elevation of the hila and tracheal deviation. The lesions also frequently calcify. These appearances are more commonly seen in patients who have had inadequately treated disease or in elderly patients who had tuberculosis before the development of chemotherapy in the 1950s.

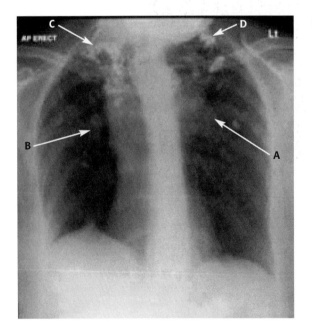

Figure 11b

An 82-year-old female presented with a five month history of right hip pain that was made worse on movement and alleviated by rest. On examination there was no obvious limb shortening but there was local tenderness over the right hip joint. The joint movement was limited on passive abduction and flexion.

Figure 12

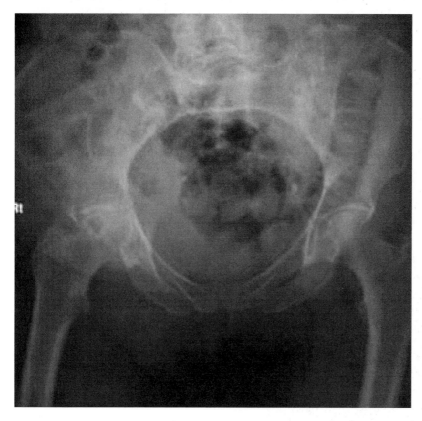

(a) *Is the film taken AP (antero-posterior) or PA (postero-anterior)?*
(b) *Describe the abnormality.*
(c) *What is the diagnosis?*

Answer

What two other radiological features are characteristic of this condition?

The film of the pelvis is taken in an antero-posterior position. The patient is lying supine on the examination table with the X-ray tube above the patient and the imaging cassette underneath the patient. The terms AP and PA refer to the position of the X-ray source and the imaging device relative to the patient. By comparison a standard chest radiograph is taken in the PA position with the X-ray source behind the patient and the patient standing with the front of the chest against the cassette.

There is degenerative change in the right hip with evidence of joint space narrowing and subchondral cyst formation. No bony injury is seen.

The appearances are those of degenerative change in the hip joint leading to osteoarthritis.

Other radiological changes which may be seen are sclerosis in the subchondral bone and osteophyte formation. Osteoarthritis is characterised by joint space narrowing. This is the result of progressive destruction and loss of the articular cartilage over the femoral head and in the acetabulum. The exposed subchondral bone becomes sclerotic and subchondral cysts occur from degenerative changes in the underlying bone. Osteophytes occur at joint margins as a response to changes in the direction of forces across the joint and are an attempt to prevent further misalignment.

Answer
overleaf

A 73-year-old lady, under the care of the elderly team, is being treated for a chest infection. A CXR is taken.

Figure 13

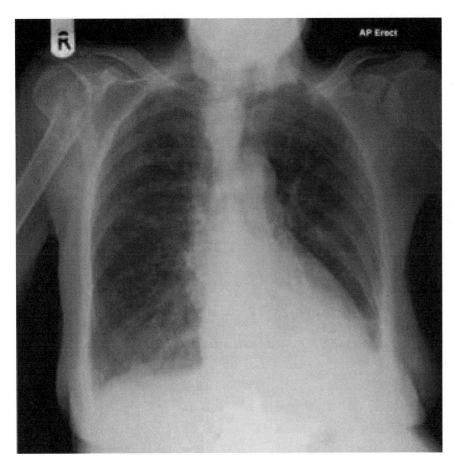

(a) *What does it show?*

Answer

There is blunting of the left costo-phrenic angle consistent with the presence of a small pleural effusion. There is also slight volume loss in the left lower zone and an air bronchogram can be seen in the left lower lobe consistent with left lower lobe consolidation although it can be difficult to assess the left lower lobe through the heart shadow.

In the right paratracheal region there is an increase in soft tissue density which represents a tortuous brachiocephalic trunk which may become prominent in the elderly.

There is a fracture of the neck of the right humerus.

This case has been included as a reminder to inspect all areas of the chest film. Remember to adopt a systematic approach to the chest radiograph looking at:

1   Heart size, contour and silhouette
2   Both hemidiaphragms
3   Mediastinal structures including aorta and trachea
4   Hilar regions
5   Lung, pulmonary vessels, lung edge
6   The areas under the diaphragm
7   Bony structures including ribs, vertebrae, and shoulder girdle.

A 70-year-old lady fell down two sets of stairs at home. She presents with severe right hip pain and is unable to weight bear. The right limb appears obviously shortened and is externally rotated at the ankle.

Figure 14a

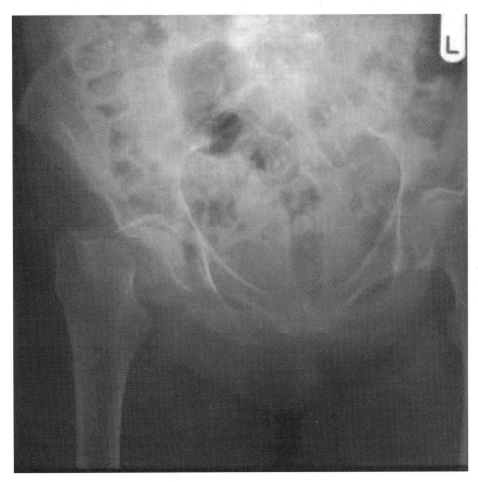

(a) *Describe the abnormality.*
(b) *What complication is likely?*
(c) *How should this be treated?*

Answer

There is a subcapital fracture of the right femoral neck.

The likely complication in this age group (especially over 65 years), is non-union of the fracture due to avascular necrosis of the femoral head. In patients under 65 years there is a dual blood supply to the femoral head inferiorly via the lateral circumflex artery and superiorly by the foveal artery. The latter vessel atrophies with time, leaving only the inferior supply. A displaced fracture of the femoral neck may tear the lateral circumflex artery and in elderly patients without the foveal artery, avascular necrosis of the femoral head may ensue. In younger individuals the foveal artery compensates for this and prevents this happening. An undisplaced fracture at any age will not damage the blood vessels and avascular necrosis should not occur.

If the femoral head is in danger of avascular necrosis a hemiarthroplasty or a total hip replacement are employed. Internal fixation may be employed if both bone fragments have an adequate blood supply although this may be difficult to assess at the time of injury.

In general internal fixation will be used in patients under 65 years. In patients over 65 years the options are a total hip replacement or replacement of the femoral head with an artificial femoral component. Total hip replacement is a more complex procedure and is reserved for patients with a high level of activity.

Figure 14b

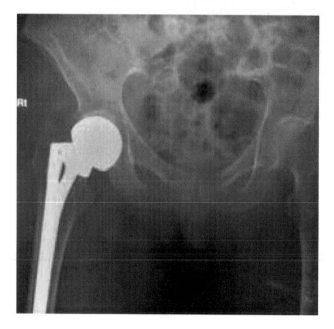

This patient underwent a right hemiarthroplasty with a femoral head replacement (Fig 14b).

A 32-year-old secretary presents with a seven month history of persistent dull back pain. She has noticed some blood in her urine and there is no history of trauma.

Figure 15

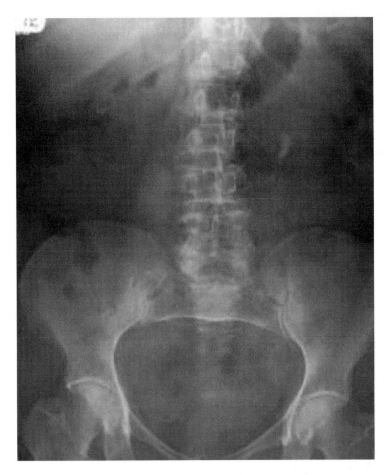

(a) *What is this examination?*
(b) *What does it show?*
(c) *What three anatomical sites are frequently affected by this condition?*
(d) *What further radiological investigation would you request and what is a possible complication of the investigation?*

Answer

This is a supine plain abdominal radiograph (sometimes referred to as a KUB: The kidneys, ureters and bladder areas should all be incorporated in the field of view.

There is an irregular shaped opacity of calcific density projected to the left of the transverse process of the 3rd lumbar vertebra. The most likely cause for this is a calculus in the lower pole of the left kidney. (Remember that the film is a two dimensional image only and the opacity could be anywhere between the X-ray source and the film.)

Renal calculi tend to occur in the calyces and at sites of narrowing in the urinary tract: the pelviureteric junction and the uretero-vesical junction.

An intravenous urogram should be considered to further evaluate the renal tracts in this patient. The most serious complication of intravenous urography is a hypersensitivity reaction to the contrast medium.

Test Paper 2

15 Questions: Time allowed 45 minutes

Answer
overleaf

A 35-year-old female presents with a history of dysphagia. Investigations include a chest x-ray and a barium swallow. The chest x-ray was taken an hour after the barium swallow had been completed.

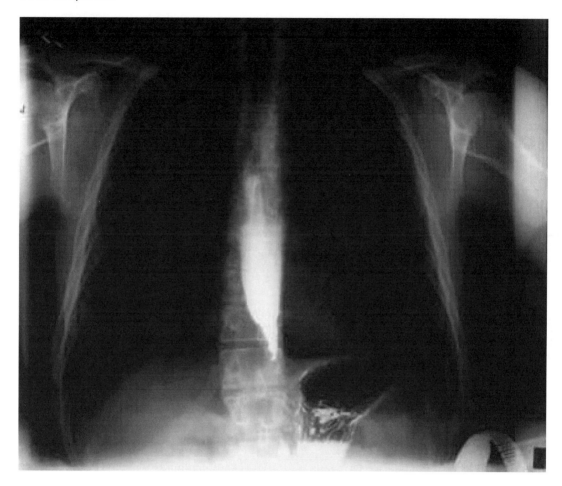

Figure 1

(a) *Why is there increased density in the mid line on the chest X-ray?*
(b) *What is the likely diagnosis?*
(c) *What are the other important causes of dysphagia?*

Answer

During a barium swallow the patient is asked to drink a liquid that contains barium. Barium is high density and shows up as white on a conventional X-ray. When a person drinks the barium, the liquid passes through the oesophagus and into the stomach in less than a minute. The chest X-ray of this patient shows that the barium is still present in the oesophagus an hour after the procedure. There is a marked delay in transit of fluid from the oesophagus into the stomach. The oesophagus is narrowed at its distal end with so called 'rat tail' tapering. This is the appearance of achalasia of the oesophagus.

This appearance mimics a stricture but it is not a true stricture; it is a tapering due to an abnormality of the muscle within the oesophagus. The tapering occurs below the diaphragm and considerable oesophageal dilatation may occur due to food in the lumen.

When considering the causes of dysphagia it is helpful to consider the anatomy of the oesophagus and neighbouring structures.

In an adult causes may be considered as follows:

Intrinsic to the oesophagus
These causes include tumours such as carcinoma, lymphoma and leiomyoma. Strictures may be due to reflux oesophagitis, ingestion with corrosives or a foreign body. Iatrogenic causes include radiotherapy and prolonged nasogastric intubation. Infection such as candidiasis can cause a painful dysphagia. Herpes simplex and CMV may also cause identical changes. Other causes include a pharyngeal web which results in a narrow anterior indentation of the upper oesophagus. (Skin disorders such as pemphigus and epidermolysis bullosa can also produce strictures).

Extrinsic to the oesophagus
Tumours in the lymph nodes of the mediastinum may cause compression of the oesophagus. Vascular abnormalities such as aortic aneurysm and right-sided aortic arch may also cause extrinsic compressions. An enlarged thyroid, prevertebral abscess or haematoma may have a similar effect.

Neuromuscular cause
Achalasia, scleroderma, Chagas disease, myasthenia gravis and bulbar pseudobulbar palsy. All these conditions affect the muscles of the oesophagus or the nerve supply to them.

Psychiatric causes
These include globushystericus.

A 55-year-old female has lower abdominal pain and complains of diarrhoea.

Figure 2

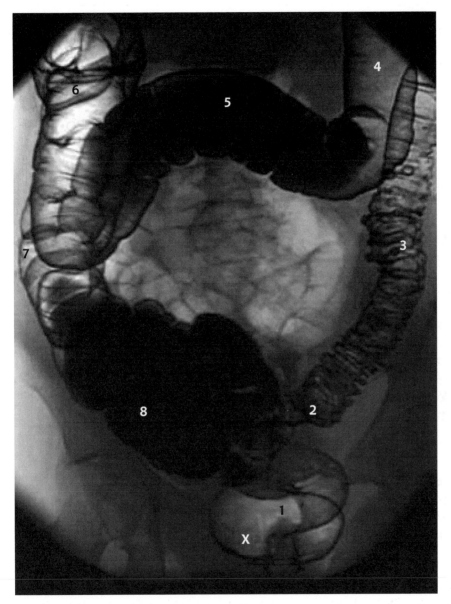

(a) *What investigation has been performed?*
(b) *How is this procedure carried out?*
(c) *Name the anatomical parts labelled one to eight.*
(d) *What is the diagnosis?*

Answer

These are digital images from a barium enema study. On digital images the contrast can be reversed so that barium which is of high density appears as black rather than white as on conventional images.

The barium enema study examines the large bowel. A rectal tube which is labelled X is inserted into the anus and rectum using lubricating jelly. The barium is introduced via the rectal tube. By getting the patient to roll onto their side the barium enters the large bowel and coats the different parts of it. The patient lies on a table which can be moved and tilting of the table is usually required to ensure adequate coating. Once the bowel is adequately coated (the radiologist checks this by screening with X-rays) the barium is drained via the tube and air is introduced to inflate the bowel. Pictures are taken of the following:

Label 1 rectum
Label 2 sigmoid colon
Label 3 descending colon
Label 4 splenic flexure
Label 5 transverse colon
Label 6 hepatic flexure
Label 7 ascending colon
Label 8 caecum.

This double contrast barium enema study demonstrates diverticular disease of the descending colon. There are diverticula throughout the descending colon which is also narrowed due to muscular spasm and hypertrophy.

A 50-year-old man has persistent focal back pain.

Figure 3a

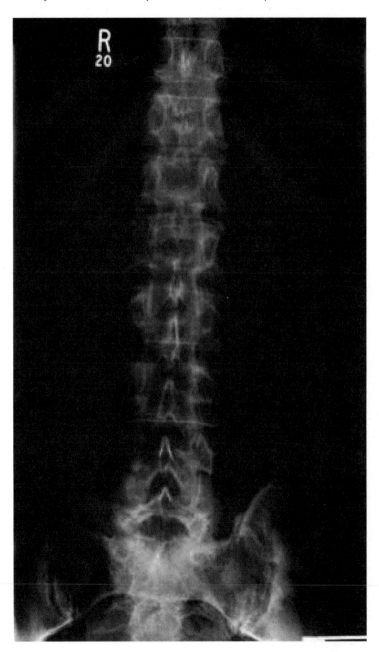

(a) *What is this investigation?*
(b) *What does it show?*
(c) *What are the causes?*

Answer

This is an X-ray of the lumbar spine. It is an AP view, ie anterior posterior view. It demonstrates destruction of the right pedicle of L2.

The most likely cause for this appearance is a metastatic deposit causing lysis or bone destruction.

Lytic bony metastases mostly arise from primary tumours of the lung and breast (but breast cancer metastases may also produce sclerosis), genito urinary tract (but not prostate which produces dense or sclerotic deposits), reproductive organs, thyroid and GI tract (stomach often causes sclerotic lesions).

Other investigations include a bone scan which involves an injection of a radioisotope. With metastatic disease there are multiple randomly scattered lesions, especially in the axial skeleton.

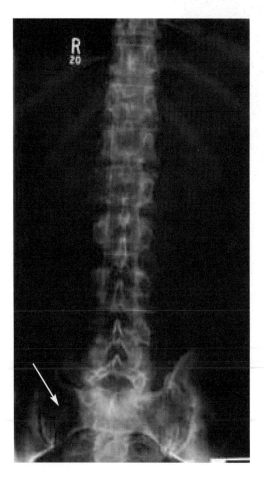

Figure 3b

A 25-year-old man has loin pain.

Figure 4

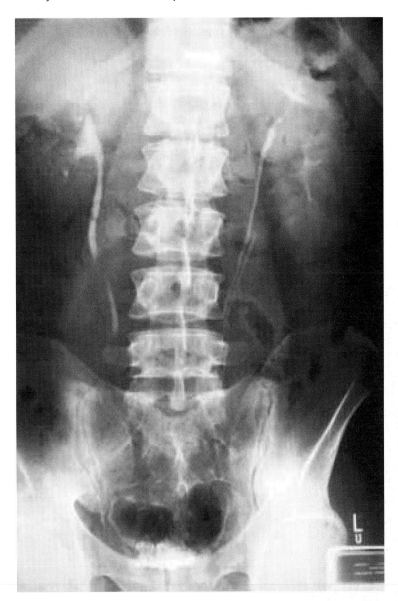

(a) *What is the investigation?*
(b) *How is it performed?*
(c) *What does it show?*

Answer

This is a film from an IVU (intravenous urogram study). As the name implies, an intravenous injection has been given to demonstrate the renal tract.

A control film is taken first. This is a plain film of the abdomen and pelvis (otherwise known as a KUB – kidney, ureter and bladder). The control film is an important part of the study and will identify calcification within the renal tract.

After checking that the control film is adequate an injection of iodinated contrast medium is administered through a vein. Compression may be applied at this stage if fine detail of the calyceal system is required. If an obstruction in the ureter is suspected, compression is not applied. A series of X-rays are performed at time intervals which depend upon the area of concern. In general by about 15 – 20 minutes contrast will be seen in the kidney, the ureters and the bladder.

This film demonstrates that contrast has entered the kidneys and is being excreted into the ureters and bladder. The contrast in the collecting system appears normal on the right but on the left there are two ureters. One ureter appears to arise from the upper part of the kidney and the other from the lower part. There is an appearance of a duplex system where there are two moieties, the upper and lower each of which is drained by a pelvis and ureter. The upper moiety ureter is prone to obstruction and the lower pole ureter is prone to reflux.

Contraindications to performing an IVU include a previous adverse reaction to iodinated contrast media, particularly if the previous reaction was severe. In some units patients with asthma are given steroid cover for the procedure as they are more likely to develop an allergic side effect.

Patients on metformin are more likely to develop lactic acidosis as a side-effect and the medication may need to be stopped before the examination. Minor effects during the procedure include an unusual, metallic taste in the mouth and a feeling of warmth around the body.

Answer overleaf

An 18-year-old woman has a chronic cough.

Figure 5

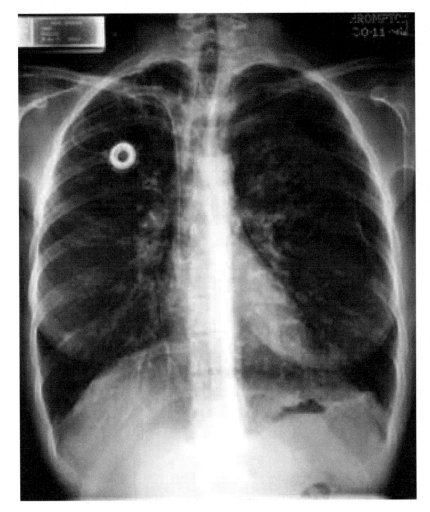

(a) *What is the investigation?*
(b) *What procedure has been performed?*
(c) *What abnormalities are shown?*
(d) *What is the diagnosis?*
(e) *What are the complications of this condition?*

Answer

This is a chest X-ray of a female patient (both breast shadows are present). A portacath has been inserted and the tip of the central venous line is projected over the right atrium. The portacath provides direct venous access and is particularly useful when patients require regular venous access on a long term basis, eg require long term antibiotics.

In both lungs there is bronchial wall thickening. There is a left-sided pneumothorax.

This patient has cystic fibrosis. Cystic fibrosis is an autosomal recessive condition in which the basic problem is one of excessively viscid mucus. The complications are as follows:

Cardiopulmonary
▮ Bronchiectasis.
▮ Current pneumonia.
▮ Focal emphysema.
▮ Pneumothorax.
▮ Cor-pulmonale.

Gastrointestinal
▮ Meconiem ileus.
▮ Thickened mucosal folds.
▮ Small bowel dilatation.

Hepatobilary
▮ Gallstones, cirrhosis.
▮ Pancreas calcification and calculi.
▮ Fibrosis and fatty replacement.
▮ Sinuses, chronic sinusitis and nasal polyps.

A 32-year-old woman presents with a lump in the right breast.

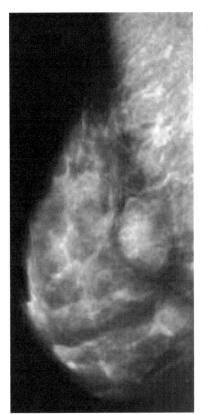

Figure 6a

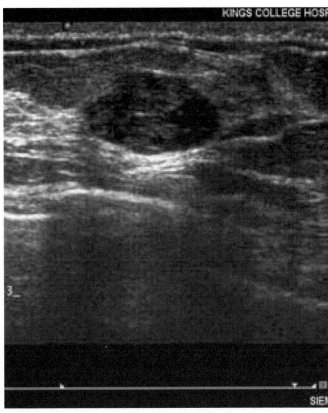

Figure 6b

(a) *What is the investigation?*
(b) *What does it demonstrate?*
(c) *What is the diagnosis?*

Answer

This is a mammogram of the right breast. A mammogram is a specialised X-ray image of the breast. Fat appears grey on the mammogram whereas glandular tissue which is denser appears white. Solid lesions in the breast may be benign or malignant. Malignant lesions have an irregular margin, are ill defined and dense (whiter than the surrounding breast). Benign lesions are well defined with a smooth contour and are less dense or have the same density as the surrounding breast.

This is an ultrasound of the breast. Ultrasound involves high frequency sound waves which enter the breast and some are absorbed but others are reflected back to the ultrasound probe and an image is formed. Cancers consist of densely packed cells and block sound wave transmission through the breast and therefore appear dark with a shadow behind them. In addition they have irregular margins, are usually taller than they are wide and may also have abnormal blood flow in them. Benign lesions, however, are horizontally orientated and do not usually block sound waves. If anything, they allow enhancement posterior to the lesion (especially cysts) and have a well defined margin or outline.

In case six the abnormality has the appearance of a benign lesion such as a fibroadenoma. This was confirmed on needle biopsy. The image below demonstrates the ultrasound guided needle biopsy. The white line through the lesion represents the needle as the biopsy is performed.

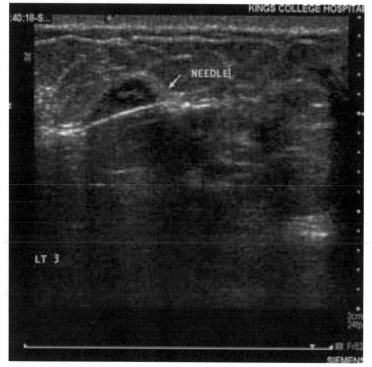

Figure 6c

Answer
overleaf

A 54-year-old lady is asymptomatic. She attends a well woman clinic and has the following tests.

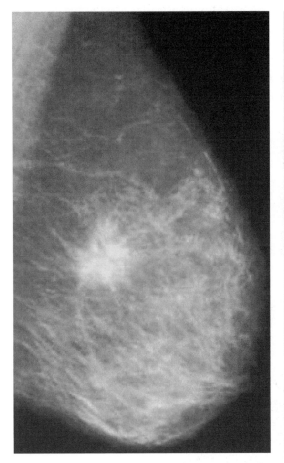

Figure 7a

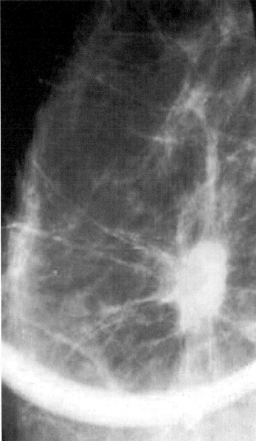

Figure 7b

(a) *What is the investigation for both images?*
(b) *What do the images show?*

Answer

(a) This is a mammogram of the left breast. It demonstrates an irregular mass in the central part of the left breast which has spicules radiating from it. The appearance is of a primary breast cancer.

(b) This image is a paddle magnification view which involves magnification and focal compression of the abnormal area only rather than the entire breast. On this view the spicules of the tumour are even more evident.

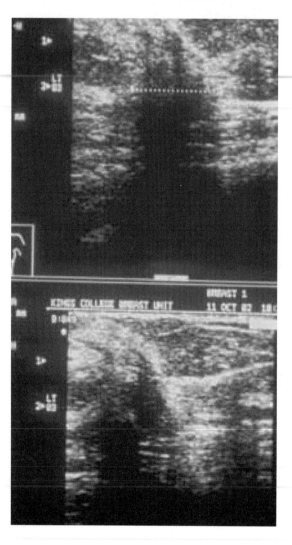

Figure 7c

This is an ultrasound of the same tumour. The lesion is hypoechoic (appears dark), is taller than it is wide and has an irregular margin.

A 45-year-old man complains of breathlessness.

Figure 8

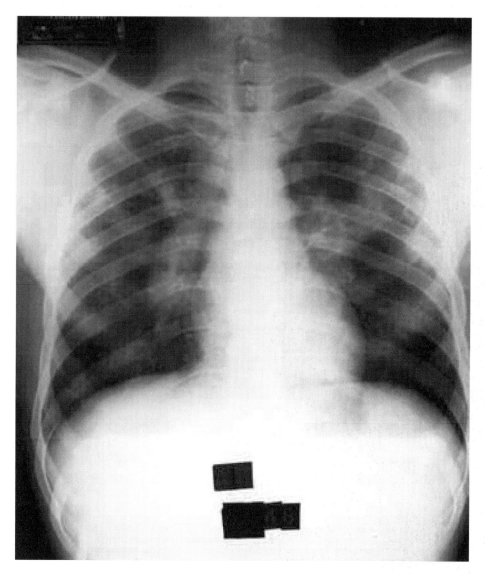

(a) *What is the investigation?*
(b) *What abnormalities are shown?*
(c) *What is the likely diagnosis?*

Answer

This is a chest X-ray taken in the PA position.

There is bilateral hilar lymphadenopathy. There are interstitial changes in both lungs but predominately in the mid and upper zones.

The diagnosis is pulmonary sarcoid. In this case this is stage three pulmonary sarcoid. Stage one is hilar lymphadenopathy alone, stage two is interstitial disease without hila lymphadenopathy and stage three is interstitial disease with hila lymphadenopathy.

Answer overleaf

A 54-year-old woman complains of breathlessness.

Figure 9

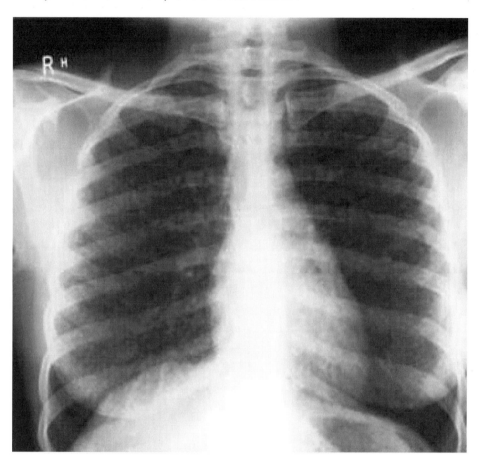

(a) *What is the investigation?*
(b) *What features are present?*
(c) *What are the possible diagnoses?*

Answer

This is a PA chest X-ray on a female patient (both breast shadows are present). There are widespread bilateral nodules in both lungs. The nodules are small (2 – 5 mm).

The causes of this appearance are sarcoid.

Metastatic disease from thyroid carcinoma, adenocarcinoma of the pancreas and breast carcinoma.

Miliary TB will also produce this appearance.

It is useful to categorise nodules according to their size. In the above example the nodules are *small* (2 – 5mm). When nodules are *medium* in size, ie 5 mm – 1 cm the diagnosis includes sarcoid and Wegener's granulomatosis. Lymphoma and metastases may also produce nodules of this size.

When nodules are *large*, ie greater than 1 cm, the most likely cause is metastatic disease. Metastatic disease to the lung is usually from the following primary tumours:

▌ breast
▌ bronchus
▌ thyroid
▌ kidney
▌ prostate.

Rheumatoid arthritis and Wegener's also cause nodules of this size.

Answer
overleaf

Figure 10a

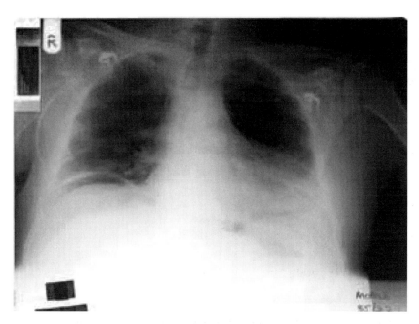

Figure 10b

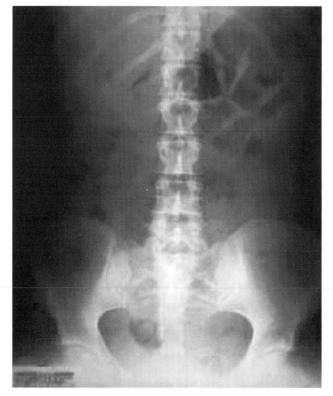

(a) *What is this investigation, what does it show and what is the significance?*
(b) *What is this investigation, what does it show and what is the significance?*

Answer

(a) This is an erect chest X-ray demonstrating the presence of free air under the diaphragm. The appearances are most obvious on the right side. The significance depends on the clinical state of the patient but usually represents a perforated abdominal viscus. It can, however, be a normal finding post-operatively, eg post – laparotomy and laporoscopy.

(b) This is a supine abdominal film which shows air outside the bowel. This is particularly evident in the left upper quadrant where there is a lucency lying lateral to the transverse colon. Air is seen on both sides of the bowel wall producing a double wall appearance and this is termed wriggler's signs. The most likely cause would be a perforated duodenal ulcer but any intra-abdominal perforation can produce this.

A 60-year-old man has severe abdominal pain and is hypotensive.

Figure 11a

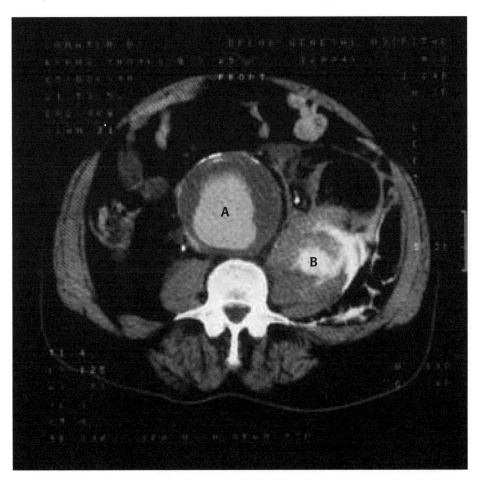

(a) *What is this investigation?*   0
(b) *How has it been performed?*   0
(c) *What does it show and what is the diagnosis?*   0

Answer

This is a CT scan of the abdomen following an injection of intravenous contrast medium ie a contrast enhanced CT scan. The contrast makes the blood appear white and anything that is actively bleeding or contains fresh blood is therefore white.

The CT scan demonstrates an enlarged abdominal aorta (b). Of significance, there is contrast leaking out of the aorta into the left psoas muscle (b). There is also some stranding and inflammation in this area. The appearances are of a dissecting abdominal aortic aneurysm. This is a surgical emergency.

Figure 11b

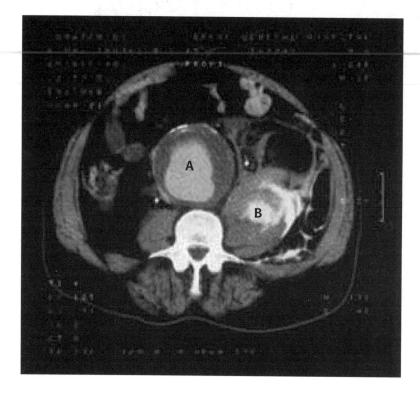

Answer
overleaf

This 50-year-old lady presents with an acute abdomen.

Figure 12

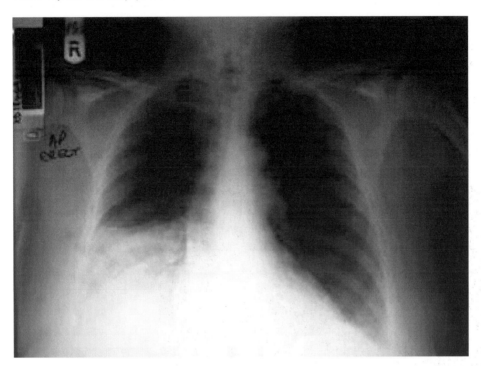

(a) *What does the chest X-ray show, what is the likely cause and how is this related to the acute abdomen?*

Answer

This chest X-ray shows opacification in the right mid and lower zones. The opacification is homogeneous and extends from the horizontal fissure to the level of the hemidiaphragm which it obscures. The features are of right middle and lower zone pneumonia.

It is important to remember that there are medical and extra abdominal causes of acute abdominal pain. The differential diagnosis includes:

▌ basal pneumonia
▌ pulmonary emboli
▌ oesophagitis or oesophageal perforation
▌ myocardial infarction
▌ thoracic aortic dissection.

Answer
overleaf

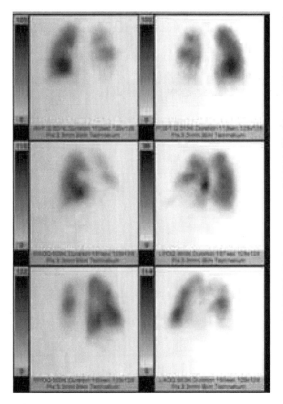

Figure 13a

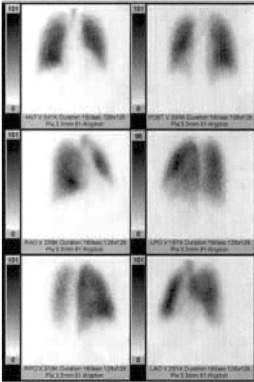

Figure 13b

(a) *What do the images in Figure 13a represent?*
(b) *What do the images in Figure 13b represent?*
(c) *What is the cause of perfusion defects?*
(d) *What is the cause of ventilation defects?*

Answer

These demonstrate perfusion images from a lung VQ (ventilation perfusion) study. There are a series of images in the:

- anterior
- posterior
- right anterior oblique
- right posterior oblique
- left posterior
- anterior oblique projections.

Perfusion abnormalities are demonstrated in the right lung.

The images from B represent ventilation scans. These can be distinguished from the perfusion scans by the presence of radioisotope centrally in the trachea. This is because radioisotope is inhaled and enters the trachea whereas with the perfusion scan it is injected into the vein. In this case the ventilation scan does not show a significant defect.

When the perfusion defects are greater than the ventilation defects one must consider pulmonary embolus as the most likely diagnosis, especially if it is multiple and segmental. Tuberculosis may typically affect an apical segment but in general tumours and infection cause a matched defect or a defect where the ventilation is more affected than the perfusion.

The ventilation defect is greater than the perfusion defect with chronic obstructive airways disease, pneumonia, lung collapse of any cause, pleural effusion and also carcinoma.

Answer overleaf

Figure 14a

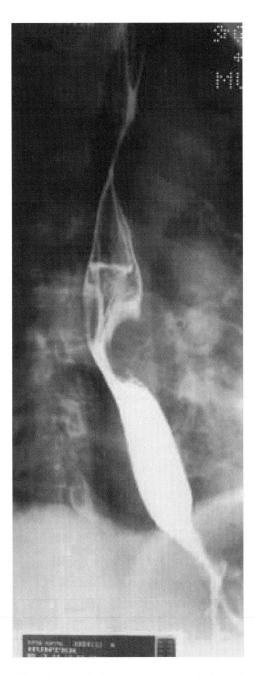

(a) *What is this investigation, how it is performed, what are the indications for this study, what are the abnormal features shown, what is the likely diagnosis?*

Please also refer to Case 1.

Answer

This is a double contrast barium swallow. The usual indications are dysphagia but occasionally it is performed to define anatomy, eg before or after surgery.

This barium swallow demonstrates a large filling defect in the mid oesophagus. The appearances suggest that the oesophagus is compressed from outside the lumen rather than from within it. The causes have been covered in the answer to Case 1. The diagnosis in this case was a leiomyoma of the oesophagus. Further imaging can be performed with a CT scan. The image below demonstrates the soft tissue mass in the oesophagus.

Figure 14b

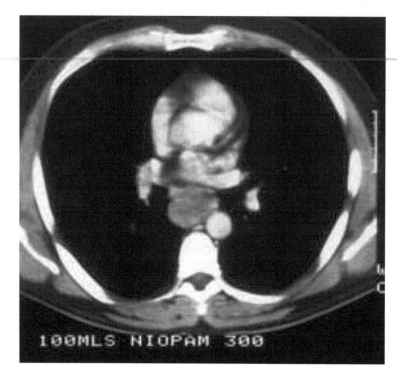

Answer
overleaf

This is an X-ray of the lower lumbar spine/sacrum and sacroiliac joints.

Figure 15

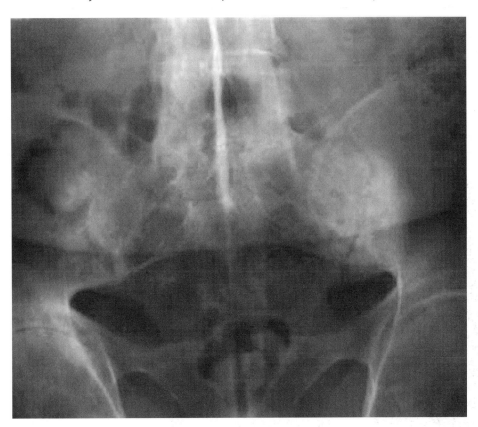

(a) *What appearances are shown and what is the likely cause?*

Answer

There is calcification and ossification of the posterior longitudinal ligament.

There are changes in both sacroiliac joints.

This patient has ankylosing spondylitis. Ankylosing spondylitis is a mesenchymal disease which mainly presents as an inflammatory arthritis affecting synovial and cartilaginous joints and also produces an enthesopathy. The axial skeleton is involved in 70 – 80% with initial changes in the sacroiliac joints followed by the thorocolumbar and lumbo sacral regions.

The appearance in the sacroiliac joints depends on the stage of the disease. Initially the lower and middle thirds of the joint are affected, particularly the iliac side. Osteoporosis and erosions may occur. Further erosion actually leads to widening of the joint space but then subchondral sclerosis and inflammation cause loss of the joint. Ankylosis, ie bone fusion then occurs.

Changes in the spine consist of osteitis which is an inflammation resulting in squaring of the vertebral body. Syndesmophytes are thin vertical bony outgrowths at the side of the vertebrae which connect the vertebral bodies to one another, resulting in the appearance of a bamboo spine.

Extra skeletal complications/associations include:

■ iritis
■ pulmonary fibrosis (upper lobe)
■ heart disease (aortic incompetence conduction defects and pericarditis)
■ amyloidosis
■ inflammatory bowel disease.

Test Paper 3

15 Questions: Time allowed 45 minutes

A patient is brought in to hospital with multiple trauma.

Figure 1

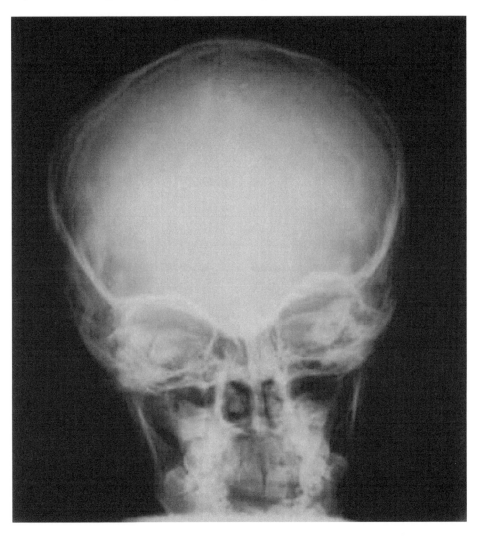

(a) *What is this study?*
(b) *What does it show?*

Answer

(a) This is a frontal (AP) skull X-ray.

(b) It shows a fracture through the right petrous temporal bone.

Answer
overleaf

A 45-year-old man is brought into the casualty department having choked on his meal; he is clinically stable.

Figure 2

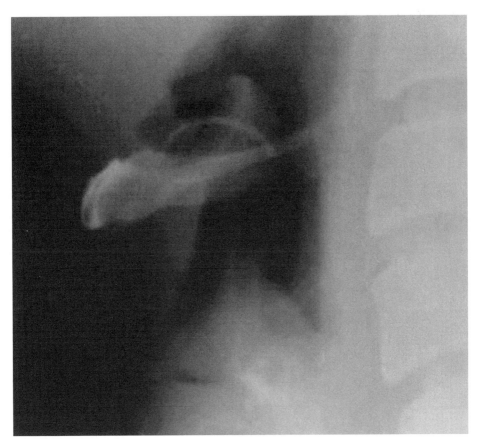

(a) *What radiological investigation do you request?*
(b) *What does it show?*
(c) *What is the cause?*
(d) *What is your management?*

Answer

(a) A lateral neck X-ray is requested.

(b) The X-ray shows a curved opacity above the hyoid bone (H).

(c) The cause is likely to be a fish bone.

(d) Referral to an ENT surgeon for endoscopy and removal of the bone.

A 72-year-old woman complains of low backache, polydipsia and polyuria. Her serum calcium is 5.3 mmol/L. A lateral spine X-ray is performed.

Figure 3a

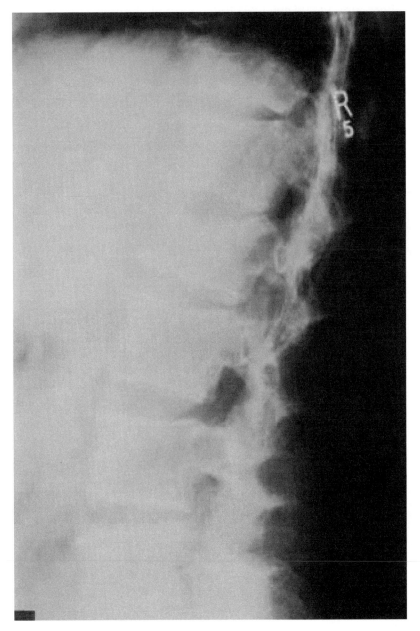

(a) *What does the X-ray show?*
(b) *What is the diagnosis?*
(c) *Which investigation will help confirm the diagnosis?*

Answer

(a) The lateral thoraco lumbar spine radiograph demonstrates loss of height of T12. The vertebral body of T12 is collapsed due to bone destruction.

(b) Bone destruction and hypercalcaemia are strongly suggestive of multiple myeloma.

(c) A serum electrophoresis, analysis of the urine for Bence-Jones proteins and a skeletal survey are helpful in making the diagnosis.

The lateral skull X-ray, (left) is part of the skeletal survey. It shows multiple small well defined punched lytic lesions which are typical of multiple myeloma.

Figure 3b

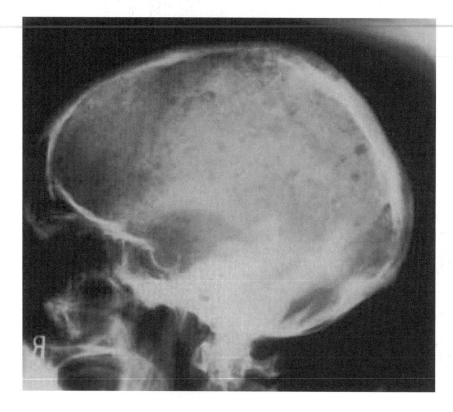

Answer
overleaf

A 20-year-old male presents with headache and reduced conscious level following an accident on his motorbike.

Figure 4

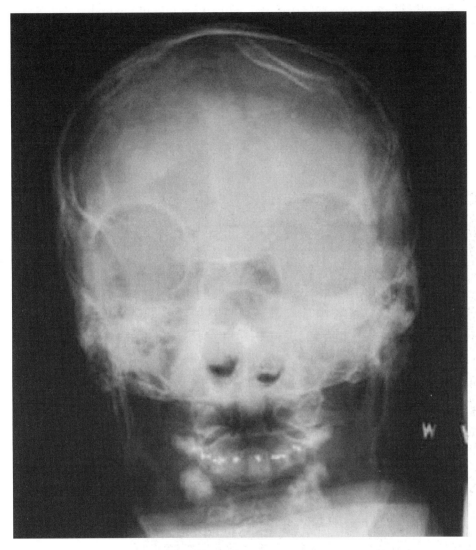

(a) *What does his skull X-ray show?*
(b) *What is the diagnosis?*

Answer

(a) There are two well defined curvilinear densities on the right side of the frontal skull X-ray.

(b) This is the appearance of a depressed skull fracture. More usually, a skull fracture appears lucent as the cortex is breached. However when a fracture is depressed, the cortex overlaps, producing an increase in density.

Answer overleaf

A 30-year-old male patient presents with progressive shortness of breath. He has a restrictive defect on lung function tests.

Figure 5

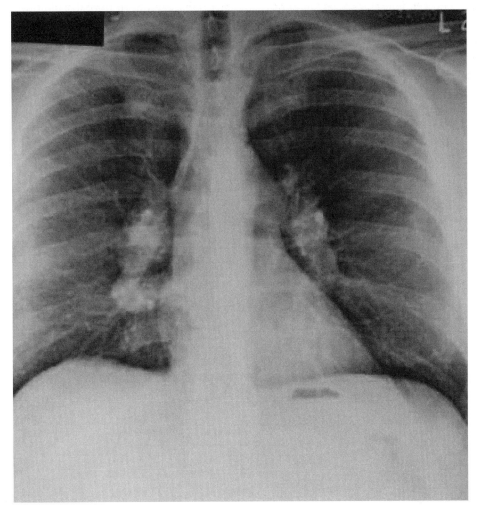

(a) *What does his chest X-ray show?*
(b) *What is the differential diagnosis?*

Answer

(a) The frontal chest radiograph shows bilateral, symmetric enlargement of the hilar lymph nodes.

(b) The differential diagnosis includes sarcoid, lymphoma and TB. Sarcoid is the most likely, especially in view of the lung function tests. Lymphoma is usually asymmetrical and other nodes, eg para-tracheal nodes, may be present. TB is rarely symmetrical. As an approximate guide the hilum should not measure more than 15 mm in a female and 16 mm in a male.

A 23-year-old male patient presented to casualty following a road traffic accident in which he sustained pelvic fractures. He required 15 units of blood and immediate surgery, after which he was transferred to the intensive care unit. Two days later he became progressively more short of breath.

Figure 6

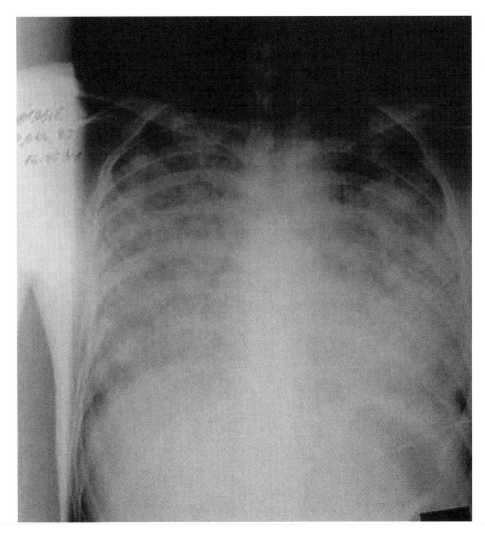

(a) *What does his chest X-ray show?*
(b) *What are the possible causes?*

Answer

(a) This is a portable chest film. ECG lines are projected over the chest wall. There is extensive bilateral ill-defined symmetric opacification with air bronchograms, ie there is widespread consolidation.

(b) The differential diagnosis for this appearance is wide and includes pulmonary oedema, infection (including atypical infections) and haemorrhage. In the context of recent trauma, adult respiratory distress syndrome (ARDS) should be considered. This is a type of noncardiogenic pulmonary oedema (cardiac failure is NOT the cause of the pulmonary oedema). Note the normal heart size on this film (cardiac function is normal).

Answer
overleaf

A 25-year-old patient with a known neurological disorder presents with headaches. The films below were taken as part of a series.

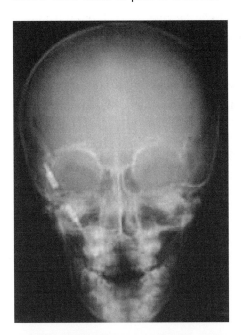

Figure 7a

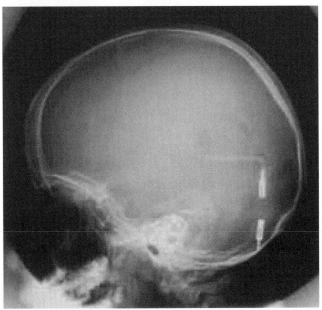

Figure 7b

(a) *What is the significance of the headaches?*
(b) *What do the films show?*
(c) *What other films are needed to complete the film series?*

Answer

(a) The headaches are a symptom of raised intracranial hypertension.

(b) The frontal skull X-ray shows that the patient has a right-sided shunt.

(c) Shunt failure can cause hydrocephalus and a rise in intracranial pressure. A shunt series examines the shunt from its origin in the ventricles to its termination which is either in the right atrium or more commonly in the peritoneum. In the latter, for example, a series would include the skull, neck, chest and abdomen to look for discontinuities, suggesting the shunt had come apart. The appearance of this shunt is normal and it is not, as many think, fractured in the region of the orbit; this is due to that part of the tubing being radiolucent. A broken shunt appears more irregular. A shunt series will not provide information on whether the shunt is blocked or infected.

An elderly patient with deafness presents with pain over his forehead. On examination there is an irregular contour over the frontal bone.

Figure 8

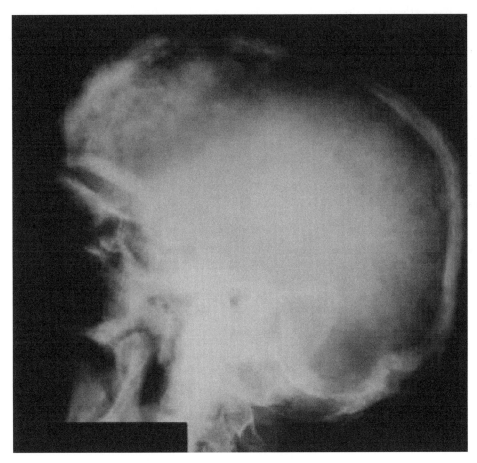

(a) *What does the X-ray show?*
(b) *What is the condition?*
(c) *What complication has arisen?*
(d) *Why is the patient deaf?*

Answer

(a) The lateral skull radiograph demonstrates cortical expansion with an increase in the skull thickness and density.

(b) These features are suggestive of Paget's disease.

(c) There is an additional area of abnormality in the frontal bone where there is a marked increase in density and irregularity of the cortex. This is suggestive of malignant transformation into an osteosarcoma.

(d) The patient is deaf because the skull base softens due to the abnormal modelling and basilar invagination occurs, compressing cranial nerves.

Answer
overleaf

A 67-year-old male patient presents with pain in his upper cervical spine. He is currently being treated for prostatic cancer.

Figure 9

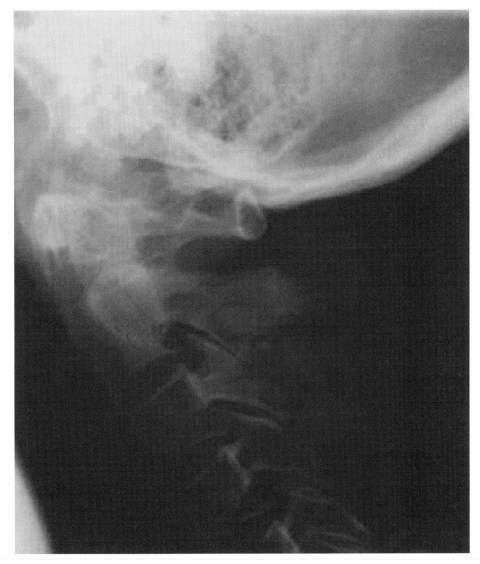

(a) *What does the cervical spine X-ray show?*
(b) *What are the possible causes?*

Answer

(a) This is a very difficult film; it is a lateral view of the cervical spine and it demonstrates an increase in density and expansion of the pedicle and spinous process of C3.

(b) Causes for this appearance include metastatic deposits from prostatic cancer and breast cancer, which are the most important causes of sclerotic metastases. Most other metastases tend to be lytic. Lymphoma can cause sclerosis, but tends not to cause expansion. Paget's disease can also cause this appearance.

A 64-year-old patient is admitted for elective repair of an inguinal hernia. The house officer thinks she can feel a pulsatile abdominal mass and asks the registrar to examine the patient. The registrar thinks that the mass is expansile as well as pulsating.

A   *What should be done next?*

Answer

Most surgeons would delay surgery until an ultrasound of the abdominal aorta had been carried out. Ultrasound is the best modality for diagnosing and following up the size of abdominal aneurysms. Much attention is paid to the size as it is of prognostic significance. If the cross-section of the abdominal aorta is more than 5 cm in AP diameter, there is a high risk of rupture. The normal maximum diameter varies from about 3 cm at the xiphisternum to about 1 cm at the bifurcation. Most patients with an aneurysm size less than 5 cm can be followed up with yearly ultrasound scans. An increase in diameter of one or more cm per year also indicates a significant probability of rupture.

The patient is put on the waiting list for repair of his aneurysm.

Answer overleaf

The patient described in question 10 goes on holiday having made a good recovery after his hernia repair. He develops acute abdominal pain and is taken to a local hospital. Unfortunately he cannot give a history to the doctors. Non-steroidal anti-inflammatory drugs are found in his pocket (he has been taking them for occasional pains following his hernia repair. His blood pressure is 70/40 mmHg and pulse is 110/min. The doctors think he may have perforated a peptic ulcer and request an erect chest X-ray and supine abdominal radiograph.

Figure 11

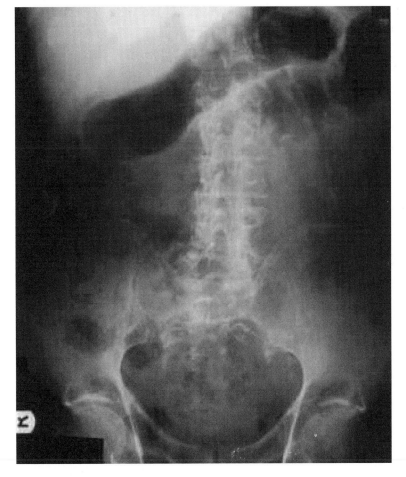

(a) *What does the abdominal X-ray show?*
(b) *What is the management?*

Answer

(a) The chest X-ray is normal; the abdominal X-ray shows calcification in the descending aorta. Calcification in a normal aorta should be just to the left of the midline. In this patient it is markedly displaced to the left because the aorta is dilated due to the aneurysm.

(b) The patient should be taken to theatre immediately, for repair of a ruptured abdominal aortic aneurysm.

Unfortunately the significance of the aortic calcification is not appreciated. However, the patient responds well to treatment with blood and plasma expanders and it is felt that the patient is stable enough to have a CT scan.

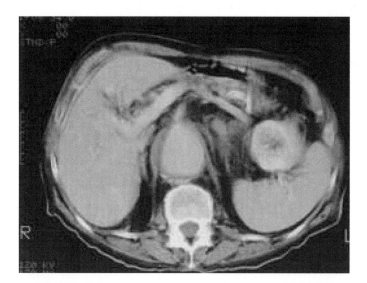

Figure 12a

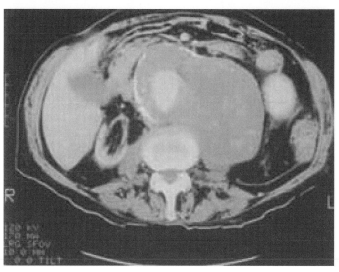

Figure 12b

(a) *What has been given to the patient to help interpretation of the scan?*
(b) *What does the first image show?*
(c) *What does the second image show?*
(d) *What is the diagnosis?*
(e) *What is the management?*

Answer

(a) Intravenous contrast medium has been given to the patient to show up blood flow in the aorta and to help determine if blood and hence contrast material is leaking out of the aorta.

(b) The first image shows calcification in the wall of the aorta. There is high density (white) material in the centre corresponding to blood in the lumen of the aorta.

(c) The second image demonstrates a large mass in continuity with the aorta. In addition, there is some high density contrast in this mass implying a leak from the aorta.

(d) The diagnosis is a ruptured abdominal aortic aneurysm.

(e) The patient should be taken to theatre immediately, for repair of the aneurysm with an aortic gift.

A 44-year-old woman presents with a week's history of a painful swollen left leg. Ten days previously she had an operation to remove her varicose veins.

(a) *What is the likely diagnosis? What are other possibilities?*
(b) *Which radiological tests could help with your management?*

Answer

(a) The likely diagnosis is a deep vein thrombosis. Risk factors include recent surgery, immobility, a long aeroplane journey, oral contraceptives, hypercoagulable states such as malignancy, polycythaemia, connective tissue disorders and clotting factor inhibitor deficiencies. Other causes of a swollen leg include oedema, eg from cardiac failure (tends to be bilateral) lymphoedema, eg malignant or infective involvement of pelvic/inguinal nodes.

(b) Traditionally, venography was used to diagnose a deep vein thrombosis. However, it is invasive and involves irradiation. Ultrasound has now become the first line of radiological investigation. Features on ultrasound that suggest a DVT include:

▌ expansion of the vein
▌ echogenic thrombosis
▌ lack of blood flow on Doppler imaging
▌ lack of variation of flow with respiration, calf compression, Valsalva manoeuvre.

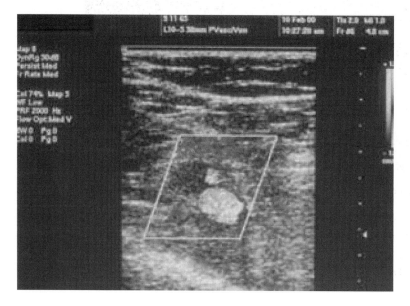

Figure 13a

The ultrasound shows uniform colour in the femoral artery but not in the common femoral vein (above and medial to the artery). The combination of clinical suspicion, the level of D dimers and the ultrasound findings are used to assess the need for anticoagulation in most hospitals now.

Ultrasound is not very accurate at excluding below knee DVT's, but it is usually not necessary to treat these as they are unlikely to embolise and the side-effects of anticoagulation outweigh the risk of pulmonary embolism from a below knee DVT.

A 45-year-old patient presents with worsening headaches. On examination he has a bitemporal hemianopia.

Figure 14a

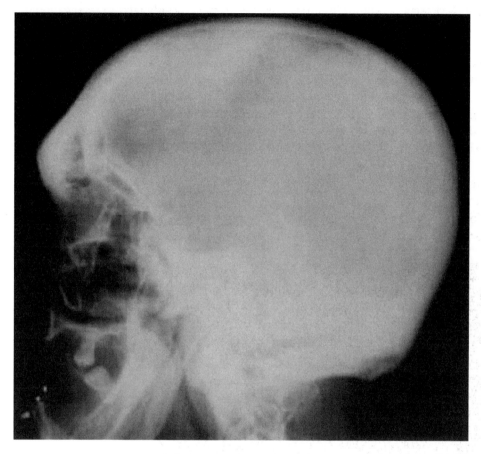

(a) *What does his skull X-ray show?*
(b) *What is the likely diagnosis?*
(c) *Which other X-rays would be useful?*
(d) *What is the management?*

Answer

(a) The lateral skull view demonstrates an enlarged cranium with prognathism (elongation of the jaw).

There is also enlargement of the pituitary fossa (sella), due to a pituitary tumour. Compare this radiograph in the question with the normal pituitary fossa shown here.

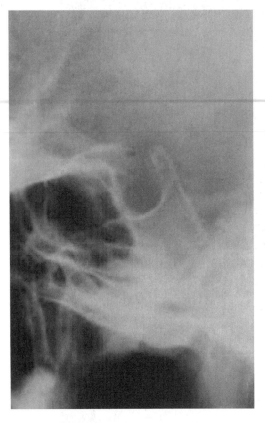

Figure 14b

(b) The diagnosis is acromegaly, which causes overgrowth of soft tissue, bones and internal organs.

(c) An X-ray of the hands would show enlarged, spade-like hands with widening of the terminal tufts.

A frontal skull X-ray may show enlarged frontal sinuses. An X-ray of the heel may show a heel pad thickness greater than 25 mm due to soft tissue overgrowth.

(d) The patient should be referred to an endocrinologist and an MRI of the pituitary requested to examine the pituitary gland.

Answer overleaf

A 22-year-old male presents to casualty having twisted his right ankle in a basketball match. On examination he is extremely tender over the base of the fifth metatarsal. The casualty officer is concerned that he may have a fracture at this site and requests a view of the foot.

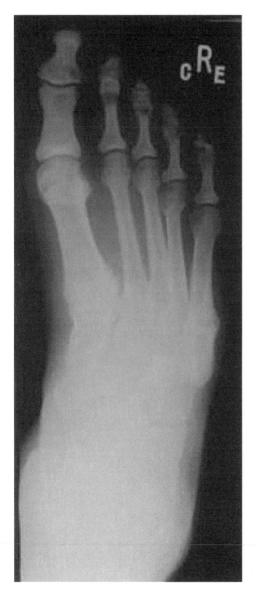

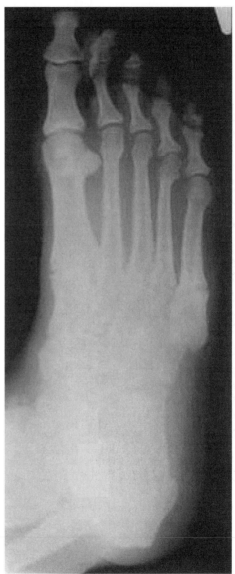

Figure 15a

Figure 15b

(a) *Look at the X-ray; is the casualty officer correct?*
(b) *What is the diagnosis?*
(c) *What is the management?*

Answer

(a) The X-ray shows a fracture across the base of the fifth metatarsal. Unlike acute fractures, this fracture line has surrounding sclerosis (increased bony density) which implies it is chronic. This site, in particular, is the site of stress in many sports and delayed union or non union or repeated fracture due to continuing stress is quite common.

(b) The diagnosis is a stress fracture.

(c) The recommended treatment is immobilisation and avoidance of weight-bearing until the fracture heals.

INDEX

femoral heads *continued*
 osteoarthritis 203–4
 replacement 208
 slipped femoral capital epiphyses
  161–2
femoral hernia xviii
femoral neck fracture 147–8, 207–8
fever 59
fibroadenoma 224
fibrosing alveolitis 57–8
flexible sigmoidoscopy 35, 36
flexion injury 137–8
foot infection 103
foot pain 189
fractures
 Colles' 139–40, 143–4
 distal radius 151–2
 femoral neck 147–8, 207–8
 greenstick 151–2
 humerus 205, 206
 insufficiency 81–2
 Monteggia's 139–40
 non-accidental injury 177–8
 pelvic 255
 radial neck 153–4
 scaphoid 145–6
 skull 111–12, 135–6, 245–6,
  251–2
 stress 189–90, 273–4

gait abnormality 125
galactorrhea 123
gallstone ileus 5–6
gallstones 19–22, 25–6
gangrene 103–4
gastrectomy 23, 24
gastric carcinoma 43–4
glioma 173–4
glucosuria 191, 192
gout 184
greenstick fractures 151–2

haematuria 27, 29–30, 31, 33, 209
haemoptysis 59

haemorrhage
 extradural 111–12
 intracerebral 113–14
 subarachnoid 107–8
 subdural 109–10
head injury 109, 111, 135–6, 245–6,
 251–2
headaches 107, 115, 127, 173, 251,
 257, 271
hearing loss 127, 259
heart x
heart disease 75
hemianopia 271
hemiarthroplasty 208
hernia
 hiatus 47–8
 inguinal xviii, 7–8, 263
hila xi
 lymphadenopathy 227–8
hip replacement 208
hips *see* femoral heads
Horner's lesion 65
humerus 205, 206
hyaline membrane disease 165–6
hydrocephalus 258
hypercalcaemia 249, 250
hyperechoic lesions 25–6
hyperparathyroidism 83–4
hypertrophic osteoarthropathy (HOA)
 87–90
hypochondrial pain 21, 29

ileo-colic intussusception 175–6
ileum xv
 Crohn's disease 49–50
 obstruction xviii, 3–4, 7–8
iliac crests xvii
iliac fossa pain 37
inappropriate behaviour 181
incontinence 125
infertility 123
inguinal hernia xviii, 7–8, 263
injury *see* trauma
insufficiency fracture 81–2